Why *Good News* People Live *Bad News* Lives

Sermons for an Emerging Church

Paul Veliyathil

Florida USA

Also by Paul Veliyathil

God is Plural

Sermons for an Emerging Church

Preface

Paul, who I have known for decades, is the type of Christian that I admire. He is one of those who not only took the time and effort to study the teachings of Jesus, but one who went beyond, and meditated deeply upon them. He is one of those who didn't simply accept everything that he was told without questioning, but one who used his God-given intelligence to examine, reflect, and reach inspired conclusions. He took the time to connect, communicate and commune with the Divine. He took the time to listen to God. And because he did all this, he went through that radical transformation that Christ calls all of us to go through. The result is generosity, patience, kindness, and compassion in motion. Paul walks the talk. Just by being who he is, he is a blessing to the world. But, moreover, he gives an enormous contribution to humanity by sharing, through his preaching, all the revelations that he was blessed with.

I invite you to savor his sermons with an open mind. Accept the challenge to use your brain and consciously question what you have, up to this moment, unconsciously accepted. What you are about to read may lead you to that radical transformation, the one that will bring you closer to God, and allow you to experience Heaven, right here on Earth.

Enjoy!

Piero Falci, Author of, *Pay Attention! Be Alert! Discovering Your Route to Happiness.*

Introduction

In an episode of *Dr. Phil* on teen parenthood, I saw this troubling scene of a 17 year old boy and a 16 year old girl with their one month old baby in the boy's lap. I consider it troubling because these teens have callously forfeited their opportunity to be children and have forced themselves to the roles of parents, for which they are neither ready nor prepared. It portends trouble both for the teens and the child and society at large.

An incredulous Dr.Phil asked them: "What were you *thinking*"? and the boy sheepishly answered: "I guess we were not *thinking*..."At least that is an honest answer. Of course, they were not thinking about the consequences and ramifications of their behavior that resulted in the unplanned pregnancy and the baby.

What was President George W. Bush thinking when he decided to invade Iraq? What was President Clinton thinking when he fooled around with an intern in the oval office? What were Governors Mark Sanford and Elliot Spitzer thinking when they engaged in sexual relations outside their marriage? What were the high-jackers thinking when they boarded those air planes on September 11, 2001? What is an enraged husband thinking when he hires someone to kill his wife? What was Bernie Madoff thinking when he was cheating his investors?

The answer is that none of them were THINKING...or at least not thinking right. In all these cases, *emotions* over-rode *thinking*. Numerous personal, national and international tragedies could have been avoided if the individuals behind them had used their brains before engaging in the behaviors that resulted in those tragedies.

I believe that the brain is the least used organ in our body. A car has many parts, but the most vital part of a car is its engine. The alloy wheels are not going anywhere, if the engine doesn't start.

The leather seats are just stagnant luxury under a metallic roof without the engine. It is the engine that makes everything alive and moving; it is the engine that makes it a car.

It is the same with our brains. We have hands and feet, eyes and ears, lungs and heart, but it is the brain that holds them all together in harmony and makes them work together.

When our mind is gone, we stop living; we may exist, but we won't live. The case of Alzheimer's patients is a clear example of this. I have many such patients on my hospice team. I had a patient who was a Harvard graduate, a classmate of Supreme Court justice Ruth Bader Ginsburg. She was a federal judge in Jacksonville. After being diagnosed with Alzheimer's, she just sat there on a wheelchair: no emotions, no meaningful expressions, no logical conversations, she didn't even recognize members of her own family.

Since our brain is the most important part of our body, how we use it determines the quality of our lives, and I mean all aspects of our lives: personal, social and spiritual. That is why William James, the most famous American spiritual writer of the 20th century said this: "The greatest discovery of my generation is that man can change his life simply by changing the attitude of his mind."

What is the brain anyway? This three pound lump of wrinkled tissue is about the size and shape of a cauliflower, and it is 85% water. This invaluable organ serves not only as the motherboard for every other system in the body, it is also the seat of your mind, your thoughts, your sense that you exist at all. You have a liver, you have your limbs, but you ARE your brain. It is the source of emotions, the repository of memory, the connection to our senses, the director of our appetites and pleasures.
(Your Body: A User's Guide, Time Inc, NY 2008)

In the last few minutes you read these paragraphs, your brain generated sixty million neurons. And a minute from now, you will have another sixty million. Of course, they are dying off at the same rate as they are generated. These neurons, along with the synapses that connect them, are the workhorses of the brain--tiny electrochemical transmitters that keep the body running.

I know a lot about these neurons and their connections, or lack thereof, because I have a son who has autism. On the outside, he looks fine. But if you interact with him you will know that something is not connecting. He cannot engage in a meaningful conversation with you because his neurons are not firing properly, or the synapses are not connecting.

Although our brain stops growing by age 20, it never stops forming new circuits as long as we live, and that is the good news. We have to stretch the brain on a daily basis. We have to use the brain for which it was created, which is to THINK. Research has shown that just using the brain actually increases the number of dendric branches that interconnect brain cells.

The more we think, the better our brains function--regardless of age. Even in old age, it can grow new neurons. Most age-related losses in memory or motor skills simply result from inactivity and a lack of mental exercise and stimulation. In other words, use it or lose it.

The human brain is able to continually adapt and rewire itself. A simple exercise like switching the hands to eat or control the computer mouse can strengthen neural pathways and even create new ones.

You can try other neural building exercises with everyday movements. Use your opposite hand to brush your teeth, dial the phone or operate the TV remote.

There is a whole area of brain exercise called *Neurobics* like Aerobics. It is a system of brain exercises using the five senses and the emotional sense in unexpected ways to shake up your everyday routines.

For example, get dressed with your eyes closed, or share a meal with only visual cues, no talking. Or break routines: go to work driving a different route, shop at a different grocery store, worship at a different church, try a different food, eat with the opposite hand.

Reading is another uniquely useful exercise to stimulate the brain along with other obvious ones like doing crossword puzzles, playing scrabble, learning a new language, etc. Watching less TV is good for your brain. When you watch TV, your brain goes into neutral.

Even walking benefits brain because it increases blood circulation and more oxygen and glucose reaches the brain. Studies have shown that inactive individuals are more likely to develop Alzheimer's compared to those with high levels of activity.

So far, I have been talking about the physical benefits of brain use. Let me touch briefly on the psychological and spiritual benefits. I firmly believe that "Life is a tragedy for those who feel and a comedy for those who think." What it means is that, instead of reacting hastily and emotionally to circumstances and events around us, if we really slow down and think through them and then act, not *re-act*, a lot of things will turn out very differently.

Crimes such as rape or murder are called "crimes of passion" because the perpetrators have not thought about the consequences of their actions. Most of the troubles human beings get into can be avoided if only they use their brains.

On a national level, I think the Iraq war was based on emotions rather than reason. It was launched at the height of our raw emotions about the events of 9/11 without thinking through its cost and consequences. I don't have to tell you how tragic it has turned out to be for both the United States and Iraq.

Our mind has a very important role to play in our spiritual life too. However, when it comes to religion and faith, many people are reluctant or even afraid to use their brains. I hear people say, "We have to take it on faith; we are not allowed to ask questions or challenge our sacred traditions." There is a bumper sticker that says: "God said it, I believe it and that settles it."

A bumper sticker faith is often a dead faith, which rarely transforms life because such a believer has not seriously thought about the meaning of what he believes. Along with Thomas Aquinas, I am interested in a faith that seeks understanding.

If you don't understand what you believe, you are unlikely to have experienced it, and if you have not experienced it, it is unlikely to change your life. Socrates said that "an unexamined life is not worth living;" and I say, "An unexamined faith is not life changing."

It is my opinion that many people are carrying in their heads a collection of socially and religiously reinforced beliefs without engaging their mind or processing them through their brain. For example, last year, a Baptist minister from Texas, Rev. Robert Jeffress, made the following statement at the *Values Summit* in Washington, D.C: "Hinduism, Buddhism, Islam and Mormonism are all, false religions." It is the most ignorant and unintelligent statement anyone with half a brain should make in this era of multiculturalism and globalization.

According to Martin Luther King Jr., *Rarely do we find men who willingly engage in hard, solid thinking. There is almost universal quest for easy answers and half-baked solutions.*

Nothing pains some people more than having to think…our minds are constantly being invaded by legions of half-truths, prejudice sand false facts.

Rev. King describes those who are unable or unwilling to think critically about their beliefs, "soft-minded" and he believes that soft-mindedness often invades religion. *The soft-minded man always fears change; he feels security in the status quo, and he has an almost morbid fear of the new. For him, the greatest pain is the pain of a new idea…soft-minded persons have revised the Beatitudes to read, "Blessed are the pure in ignorance: for they shall see God.*

And I totally agree with MLK who makes this powerful statement: *The shape of the world today does not permit us the luxury of soft-mindedness. A nation or a civilization that continues to produce soft-minded men purchases its own spiritual death on an installment plan. (Strength to Love, pp.14-17)*

I think God gave us a brain to use it, to figure out life, including our faith. In order to do that, we have to have an open mind. Our mind is like a parachute; it works only if it is open. Cultivate a mind that is open, flexible and adaptable to include the ironies, the mysteries and the contradictions of life; a mind that is capable of thinking beyond the categories of "black and white" and "either or," a mind that is not afraid to think outside the box.

Some might say that a flexible mind is a sign of weakness or lack of deep convictions. But I agree with Emerson who said that **Consistency is the mark of a mediocre mind.**

A flexible mind is capable of deep reflection and it has the capacity to engage in new and creative ways of thinking and understanding the complexities of life. Let me tell you a story. A man was on a scavenger hunt and knocks at the door of Mr. Smith. It was the middle of the night. The man tells Mr. Smith:

"I need a piece of wood, 3 x7 feet and I will pay you five thousand dollars." Mr. Smith thought for a moment; *Home Depot* and *Lowes* are closed; there is no wood in the garage. "I am sorry; I can't help you, I don't have any wood in the house."

The man leaves and Mr. Smith goes back to bed, but he can't sleep. He had all kinds of thoughts going through his mind. *If only I had bought some wood during my last trip to the Home Depot, I would have had $5000 in my hand*. He thought about all the things he could have done with that money, such as taking his wife on a cruise, down payment on a new car, etc. He felt so depressed and began to fall asleep. Suddenly, he jumped out of his bed and said to himself: *The door… the door*; he had half a dozen doors in his house, all of them made of wood, 3x7 feet. He could have given one of them to the man!

What happened here is that, when Mr. Smith heard the word "wood" he could only think of the wood on the shelves of *Home Depot*. His mind did not have the flexibility to expand and include the fact that the door was indeed wood; he had put door in the category of door only, and wood as separate from it.

We do this all the time. When it comes to life, death, God, Jesus, the Bible, salvation, etc., we have this one track mind. We are afraid, unable or unwilling to think about or include other possibilities. That is why life becomes a struggle, our faith gets stagnated, our spirituality becomes choreographed to fit the confines of one religion, our experience of God is limited to reading just one holy book, and our encounter with Jesus is often within the four walls of a church. As a result, we rarely feel the joy and freedom of the children of God.

It is so important to use our brains to explore the edges of our faith to make it relevant and meaningful for our times. It is crucial that we use our brains to make our lives meaningful.

So the purpose of this book is to emphasize the importance of thinking, and to encourage re-thinking about a lot of issues you thought you had already settled, especially in areas of theology, faith and life itself.

Even though it is a collection of sermons, there is a basic theme that is running through all of them. The major thesis of this book is that we are primarily saints not sinners, that we start our lives with original blessing rather than with original sin, that we are spiritual beings first and humans second. In Deepak Chopra's words, "we are divinity in disguise and gods and goddesses in embryo."

Our life-goal is to experience ourselves as spiritual beings, to nurture the divinity within us and ultimately express it in our daily lives and interactions. For that to happen, our *thinking* has to change first, because our thinking is at the foundation of who we are and what we do. That is why Socrates said so profoundly, *"cogit, ergo sum," I think, therefore, I am.*

So, it is all about the narrative. It is all about the story we tell ourselves. In these sermons, I am changing the traditional Christian narrative. It may disturb you and destabilize your faith. But please, bear with me and hear me out and think deeply before you dismiss them. It could change your life for the better. It did mine.

The traditional narrative of the Christian faith is that we are born in sin. As humans, we are unworthy, weak and depraved. We need a Messiah to save us from sin and grant us eternal life in heaven after we die. Jesus saves us from our sins by dying on the cross. He saves only those who confess his name. This Jesus is now sitting at the right hand of God and he will come again as a triumphant king to take believers into heaven and unbelievers will be dispatched into hell.

We have based our faith life on this narrative for centuries and nothing much has changed. We still fight wars, and there is poverty, injustice, hatred, disharmony and disunity all over the world. Some of these sins are rampant among Christians who live this narrative.

I invite you to change the above story and try to live by a different narrative.

Let us live our lives from the vantage point of being *saints* rather than *sinners*, as a people created in the image and likeness of God, called by Jesus to be perfect as his heavenly father is perfect.

Let us focus on our strengths rather than on our weaknesses by remembering that we are *co-creators* with God rather than mere *creatures,* because we are *a part* of God rather than *apart* from God.

In this narrative, we seek *empowerment* rather than *salvation*, *transformation* more than *information*.

We will live by the bible rather than merely read it or carry it around in nice leather cases. We will not get stuck on dogma and doctrines, but focus on the meaning of those doctrines and how they became part of the faith tradition.

In this narrative, we will take time to examine the handed-down beliefs of our ancestors rather than buy into them blindly.

In this narrative, we will ask the question "why am I so infrequently the person that *I am*?" rather than "why don't I become a better person?"

In this narrative, we will assume our rightful role in life as responsible adults rather than dependent victims. .

In this narrative, prayer will be less about coaxing an unwilling God for blessings, but more about basking in the blessings already given.

We will take charge of our lives instead of being discharged by life.

I know full well that changing the traditional narrative will be considered heretical and the Church always tries to conserve and bless the majority opinion. Martin Luther King Jr. once asked, *We preach comforting sermons and avoid saying anything from the pulpit which might disturb the respectable views of the comfortable members of our congregations. Have we ministers of Jesus Christ sacrificed truth on the altar of self-interest and, like Pilate, yielded our convictions to the demands of the crowd?*

And then he adds this scathing critique: *Any Christian who blindly accepts the opinions of the majority and in fear and timidity follows a path of expediency and social approval is a mental and spiritual slave. (Strength to Love, pp. 26-7)*

As a keen observer of life, I feel that many people are merely meandering through the meaningless monotony of a largely lethargic life. It doesn't have to be that way. We can awaken from the slumbering state of a wonder-less wanderer to the magical mind of a marveling mystic. I am convinced that it is possible, if only we would draw from our inner source, a largely undiscovered and untapped depository of pure goodness, holiness and bliss.

These sermons were preached first at Faith Christian Church in Hollywood, Florida and I thank the members of that congregation for their patience and fortitude in listening to me. It is my hope that these sermons will find a larger audience. I also want to thank my friend, Piero Falci, who graciously wrote the preface and my wife, Judy for patiently editing it.

I like to end this introduction with a funny story and a serious quote. First, the story.

A doctor told a man waiting for surgery. "I have got good news and bad news for you; the bad news is that you have an inoperable brain tumor; the good news is that there are two brains available for transplant; they are from a young couple killed in an accident; you can have whichever brain you like; the man's brain will cost you a $100,000 and the woman's brain, $30,000."

The patient said "If you don't mind me asking doctor, why is there such a huge difference between the price of male and female brains?" And the doctor replied: "The female brain is *used*."

And that is a shout out to women who I believe use their brains more than men. So, I like to start by re-thinking the age old notion that "women are the weaker sex." Compared to men, women may lack in muscle strength, but the strength and resilience they manifest in childbearing, parenting, and in many other areas of life, not to mention dealing with fickle and frivolous men, who eagerly stray and are easily swayed, makes them anything but weak.

As you start reading the following pages, you may feel resistance, confusion and even anger because, the ideas proposed may challenge your belief system and your long held views on life, and may even shake the foundations of your faith itself. It may not be a bad thing because as my late farmer-father used to say, you cannot grow new plants, unless you shake the ground before planting them.

Embracing a narrative that has the potential to shake the foundations of one's so-called secure faith takes enormous courage. That is why it is often said, tongue in cheek, "transformation ain't for sissies."

So, this book is an invitation to consciously unlearn what you may have unconsciously learned about religion, faith and life itself. It is a call to think first, think different, and of course, re-think old notions, and above all, a clarion call to use the brain that God gave you to navigate the complexities of our complicated lives in an increasingly complex world.

In other words, it is an admonition to reflect deeply on the Socratic dictum that an unexamined life is not worth living.

Again to put it differently, the purpose of this book is to help you wake up from the "hypnosis of social conditioning" and "live abundantly" with conscious awareness of its full potential and possibilities. Such a life is never viable with a brain that is under used or mortgaged to traditions and institutions.

Let me begin by joining Mark Victor Hansen who says: "You were born rich with eighteen billion bountiful, beautiful, totally available and in all probability under used brain cells, awaiting your desire, decision and directional compass to take you onward, upward, good ward and God ward."

Rev. Paul Veliyathil, Th.D.
Coral Springs, FL
March 31, 2013

Contents

1. The Pope and the Rabbi 18
2. Death of Common Sense 24
3. Undigested Faith 31
4. I Don't Believe in God Any More 38
5. America's Four Gods 46
6. From EGO to FROG 52
7. Does God Control Traffic Signals? 59
8. Taking the Bible Seriously, Not Literally 65
9. Think Different 72
10. Why Good News People Live Bad News Lives 79
11. Are You a CINO? 86
12. Christian or Disciple? 92
13. Adam and Eve: The Untold Story 99
14. Not Just Human 105
15. God's Xerox Copies 111
16. What God wants 117
17. From Limping to Dancing 124
18. The Fifth Gospel 131
19. Living Inside Out 137
20. Everyday Miracles 145
21. Significance of Insignificance 152
22. Re-thinking Heaven 159
23. From Stressed to Blessed 165
24. We Belong to Each Other 173
25. Is it True, Is it Necessary and Is it Kind? 181
26. Holy Ground versus Stand Your Ground 188
27. Are You Joyful? 195
28. Live in the Moment 202
29. MAGIC Formula for the New Year 210
30. Judgment-free Zone 217

1. The Pope and the Rabbi
Text: Mathew 16: 13-16

When Jesus came to the region of Caesarea Philippi, the asked his disciples, "Who do people say the Son of Man is"? Thy replied, "Some say John the Baptist; others say Elijah; and still others, Jeremiah or one of the prophets." "But what about you" he asked. "Who do you say I am?" Simon Peter answered, "You are the Christ, the Son of the living God."

Several Centuries ago, the Pope decreed that the Jews had to convert to Catholicism or leave Italy. There was a huge outcry from the Jewish community. So the Pope offered a deal. He'd have a religious debate with the leader of the Jewish community. If the Jews won, they could stay in Italy; if the Pope won, they'd have to convert or leave.

The Jewish people met and picked an aged and wise rabbi to represent them in the debate. However, as the rabbi spoke no Italian and the Pope spoke no Yiddish, they agreed that it would be a silent debate. On the chosen day, the Pope and the rabbi sat opposite each other.

The Pope raised his hand and showed three fingers. The rabbi looked back and raised one finger. Next, the Pope waved his finger around his head. The rabbi pointed to the ground where he sat. The Pope brought out a communion wafer and chalice of wine. The rabbi pulled out an apple.

With that, the Pope stood up and declared himself beaten and said that the rabbi was too clever. The Jews could say in Italy.

Later the cardinals met with the Pope and asked him what had happened.

The Pope said, "First I held up three fingers to represent the Trinity. He responded by holding up a single finger to remind me there is still only one God common to both religions.

Then, I waved my finger around my head to show him that God was all around us. He responded by pointing to the ground to show that God was also right here with us.

I pulled out the bread and wine to show that the sacrifice of Jesus absolves us all our sins. He pulled out an apple to remind me of the original sin.

He bested me at every move and I could not continue."

Meanwhile, the Jewish community gathered to ask the rabbi how he'd won.

"I don't have a clue" said the rabbi. "First, he told me that we had three days to get out of Italy, so I gave him the finger."

"Then he tells me that the whole country would be cleared of Jews and I told him that we were staying right here."

"And then what?" asked a woman.

"Who knows?" said the rabbi. "*He took out his lunch, so I took out mine.*"

I love that story. It is a great story with some profound lessons.

The first lesson of this story is that "nothing has meaning except the meaning you give." If you could understand the implications of that statement, your life will change for the better; you will experience more peace and joy in your life and this world would be a much better place; there will be no more wars or poverty or conflict or arguments.

Nothing has meaning except the meaning you give. We attach meaning to events and experiences in our lives. A camera that takes a picture of a yellow bus will just take that picture, but our human eyes will look at the same yellow bus and say, it is a school bus. We attach a specific meaning to that yellow bus. Meaning making is a uniquely human ability. It is the meaning that determines the outcome. And we can attach different meaning to the same event and experience different outcomes.

Let us go back to the story. When the pope raised his 3 fingers, he meant the Trinity, but the rabbi thought it meant that the Jews had 3 days to get out of Italy. When the Rabbi raised 1 finger, he was giving the pope the finger, but the pope thought he was reminding him about the one true God.

For the pope, the bread and the wine represented the sacrifice of Jesus on the cross. For the rabbi, they represented lunch.

The point of the story is that meanings are not absolute. There is no one single, unchangeable, infallible meaning for anything in life. Events and symbols have only the meaning we attribute to them.

The fact of the matter is that **we are meaning makers**; the only thing that matters is the meaning we give. For example, on the day of Yom Kippur I will go to work, have a steak for supper, watch some TV at night and go to bed. It will be no different than any other day of my life. It is just another Friday. I say TGIF.

But for my Jewish co-worker, it is not a mere Friday on a calendar. That day is filled with religious meaning. It is the Day of Atonement; he will take off from work that day; he will fast the entire day and will not eat meat. He will observe it as a holy day.

Let me take another Friday on the calendar. I call it *Good Friday*. I will take off from work that day, will fast for the day, will not eat meat and refrain from watching sitcoms and instead watch the *Passion of the Christ*. My Jewish friend won't do any of that because Good Friday for him is just like any other Friday. He will say TGIF.

Similarly, I might look at a cow and dream of future hamburgers and steaks; but my Hindu friend will look at a cow and see God. Same reality, different meanings.

It is so instructive to reflect on the words of Shakespeare' in *Hamlet*: "Nothing is either good or bad but our thinking makes it so."

So always remember that we humans are meaning makers. The meaning making is most visible and also problematic in the area of religion. Very often, we are either reluctant or afraid to attach our own meanings when it comes to matters of faith, God, and religion. We blindly accept the meaning our forefathers gave to something and run with it, without thinking twice about it. We call it tradition.

A few years ago, I was invited to a bris. The rabbi came, recited few Hebrew prayers, did the religious surgery, collected his fee and left. And the party was great. Later, I asked the young mother of the child, who was a co-worker, as to why she had to do this ceremony today, in Coral Springs Florida, in the year 2010. She was quiet for a moment and said: "Our forefathers did it; it is a **tradition** in our religion." But she had no clue where that tradition started or what it meant. Repeating a ritual or believing a dogma for the sake of the tradition without understanding its meaning and significance for our life is called traditionalism. As Jeroslav Jan Pelikan said**, tradition is the living faith of the dead and traditionalism is the dead faith of the living.**
As a religious practice, I think circumcision is meaningless, now and even centuries ago, when it first started. According to the book of Genesis, chapter 17, circumcision was the 'seal of the

covenant' between God and Abraham. God said to Abraham that every male child had to be circumcised on the 8th day of his birth. V. 14 says: "If a male is uncircumcised, he shall be cut off from his people; he has broken my covenant."

My question is, if it is a sign of a covenant with God, what about the women? Are they not part of the covenant? Why would God want to exclude women from having a covenant with Him? That doesn't sound like a nice God to me! What about the billions of Chinese and Indian men who never undergo circumcision? Do you think all those people are outside the grace and covenant of God?

Don't just blindly accept the meaning a person or a group of persons gave to a certain statement or event, long time ago. Give your own meaning to the events and the experiences in your life. This is very crucial especially when you read Scriptures.

When you read the bible, you are reading the meaning people in biblical times gave to those events and experiences. What you read in the bible may be meaningful to you today, or it may not be. For example, most books of the Old Testament do not make much sense to me. If it does not make sense to you, it is all right to ask questions about it. It is important to investigate.

You just don't have to take it on face value and believe something just because it is printed on the pages of a holy book. Just believing because it is in the bible will not make any difference in your life, because you have neither understood its original meaning nor its current application.

For example Apostle Paul says: "Nothing can separate me from the love of Christ; neither heights, nor depths, neither principalities nor powers." That is Paul's experience as a result of his encounter with Christ on his way to Damascus. Is that your experience too? Are you just repeating it because Paul wrote it?

Because, if it is not your experience, it won't have any impact on your life. Do you feel that **nothing can separate you** from the love of Christ?

In the book of Revelations, John says: "Jesus is the Alpha and the Omega." Do you feel that way in your life, or you repeat it because John says it?

There is no shortage of copies of the bible in the world. There are millions of copies in hundreds of languages all over the world. But the world has not changed for the better. Merely reading the words in the bible won't change your lives; understanding its meaning and applying it to your life will. And it has to be the meaning you give. Just as you cannot wear somebody else's prescription glasses and expect to see anything clearly, you cannot read somebody else's words, and blindly believe it without making it meaningful to you today.

That is why Jesus gathers his disciples and asks them "Who do people say that the son of man is?" And they replied with several answers from different people: "Some say, John the Baptist, others Elijah, still others Jeremiah or one of the prophets." Jesus was not interested in what others thought of him. He wanted to know what his disciples thought. And that is why he turned to them and asked: "And you, who do you, say that I am?" And Simon Peter gave a personal answer. "You are the Messiah!" And that confession of personal meaning changed Peter's life.

I want to give you an exercise for the week. Think of some of the articles of your faith and ask yourself: Do I understand what it means? Am I just repeating it or do I really believe what it says? Do I believe it because it is meaningful to me or do I believe it because it is somebody else's meaning? Write the Apostles' Creed on a piece of paper, or print it off the internet and just read it and reflect on it and see how much sense it makes to you in your day to day life? It will indeed be a surprising discovery.

2. Death of Common Sense
Text: Matthew 12:1-14

At that time Jesus went through the grain fields on the Sabbath. His disciples were hungry and began to pick some head of grain and eat them. When the Pharisees saw this, they said to him, "Look! Your disciples are doing what is unlawful on the Sabbath."

He answered, "Haven't you read what David did when he and his companions were hungry? He entered the house of God, and he and his companions ate the consecrated bread—which was not lawful for them to do, but only for the priests. Or haven't you read in the Law that on Sabbath the priests in the temple desecrate the day and yet are innocent? I tell you that one greater than the temple is here; If you had known what these words mean, 'I desire mercy, not sacrifice' you would not have condemned the innocent. For the Son of Man is Lord of the Sabbath.

He said to them, "If any of you has a sheep and it falls into a pit on the Sabbath, will you not take hold of it and lift it out? How much more valuable is a man than a sheep! Therefore it is lawful to do good on the Sabbath." Then he said to the man, "stretch out you hand." So he stretched it out and it was completely restored, just as sound as the other. But the Pharisees went out and plotted how they might kill Jesus.

You have heard the expression, "common sense is the most uncommon thing in the world" and there may be some truth to that. I recently read a book called *The Death of Common Sense*, by Philip K. Howard. It is a book about the system of governmental regulations and how it is "suffocating America." The author argues that although we have a democratic system in this country, the laws and statutes that we have created are actually stifling people rather than making them grow.

The book provides many stories of how bureaucratic rigidity, ineffective regulation, and overly complex procedures and rules have superseded good judgment and common sense. For example, the book begins with the story of an abandoned building in New York City that was sold to the sisters of Mother Theresa for one dollar, to make it into a homeless shelter.

The code required that the building should have an elevator. It would cost the sisters an extra $100,000. The sisters were willing to walk up and down the stairs; the homeless people wouldn't have really cared whether there was an elevator in the building as long as they had a place to sleep. The irony is that it would cost $100,000 for an elevator for a building that they paid one dollar for. The city wouldn't budge. And the sisters had to abandon the project.

The author says that "in many cases, we have created a system that often precludes the exercise of common sense and judgment." You have heard of the law that baby stroller manufacturers have to follow; they have to place a label on the stroller that says: "Please remove the baby before folding the stroller."

Let me tell you another story about a Mrs. Grazinski of Oklahoma City who purchased a new 32-foot Winnebago motor home. On her first trip home, driving on the freeway, she set the cruise control at 70 mph and calmly left the driver's seat to go to the back of the Winnebago to make a sandwich. Not surprisingly, the motor home veered, crashed and overturned. Mrs. Grazinski sued Winnebago for not putting in the owner's manual a warning "Do not leave the driver's seat while the cruise control is on." A jury in Oklahoma awarded her $1,750,000 plus a new motor home! Winnebago actually changed their manuals as a result of this law suit!
Let me give you an example from my life. My son Johnny, who is autistic, turned 18 in December 2010. As far as the law is

concerned he is an adult. He has the body of an 18 year old but the mind of a 5 year old. He is totally dependent on us. But God forbid, he ends up in a hospital, the doctors don't have to share any information with us, due to HIPPA (Health Insurance Privacy and Portability Act) regulations, because, as far as the law is concerned, he is an adult and we have no rights.

So as parents, if we want to have any say about his life, we have to hire an attorney, go to court, appear before a judge and he has to grant us guardianship of our son. This is a tedious and expensive process. We have to fill out so many redundant papers. We have to attend classes and our son has to be evaluated by half a dozen professionals, and we have to spend about $5000 for attorney fees and court costs. All this to obtain guardianship of our son, whom we gave birth to and have raised for the past 18 years!

You may be wondering why I am telling you all these stories about lack of common sense during a church service. This should be a speech for a civic class. Not really. The lack of common sense is not just in government. There is a lot of it in religion too.

When we take every verse of the bible literally without thinking about the assumptions and context behind that verse, we are not using common sense; we are being childish disciples. When we follow a religious tradition for the sake of the tradition without thinking about how it applies to our current life situation, we are not using our God given common sense. We are being blind followers. Then we wonder why religion does not really transform our lives and that of society.

Let me give you some examples. Take the case of the rule of celibacy for Catholic priests. There is no biblical foundation for it. Until the 11th century, priests were married. The first 39 popes were married. Mandated celibacy for Catholic priests has a history of only 1000 years. As the Church holds on tightly to this rule, about 4000 parishes are closed down in the United States with no Sunday Mass. People are spiritually starving, but the Pope won't change the rule. The irony is that the Church welcomes married Anglican priests (with their wives and children) and makes them Catholic priests, but the Church won't take someone like me back to priesthood, because I have a wife and children! Go figure the common sense of that.

Let us examine our understanding of God. Many people still think that God has a gender and it is male; that God is separate from us and that God is 'up' there beyond the clouds. In conversations with my patients, I hear it all the time. They would point the fingers towards the sky and say: "The man up there has to decide." The notion that God is "up there" is a 2000 year old idea. The Bible was written before the age of Copernicus and Galileo who discovered that the earth is round and it revolves around the sun. He was jailed for saying that because it went against the teachings of the Bible. It took the Church 500 years to apologize to Galileo.

Let us examine our understanding of prayer from a common sense perspective. We think that we have to implore God and somehow twist the arms of a reluctant deity to give us some blessings. And we will quote Mt: 7:7 to prove it: "Ask and you will receive and seek and you will find." But then again, there is Mt: 6: 8 where Jesus says: "When you pray, do not keep on babbling like the pagans; for your father knows what you need before you ask him." Confusing, right? Here is where you have to use to your common sense to look for the context of the Bible verses and understand their deeper meaning.

There was a story about a house that was not destroyed during the tornadoes in Joplin, Missouri, a few months ago. All the houses around were destroyed, but this one house stood there relatively intact, except for some roof damage. The owners were interviewed about their response to this event. This lady, obviously a Christian, said: "God heard our prayers; we thank the Lord for protecting us." What about the prayers of the people in the neighboring houses? God didn't hear their prayers? Maybe they didn't use the right prayer? Maybe they didn't pray to the right God? Why would a God who created all the people, spare some and punish others? It makes no sense. No wonder people are confused about what prayer really means and how it works!

Let us examine our understanding of salvation. Many Christians believe that only those who profess Jesus as their personal savior will be saved. Think about that for a moment. There are nearly 7 billion people on this planet. About three billion of them are Christians. By the way, according to the Jehovah's Witnesses, only 144,000 will be saved. I am not sure how they came up with that exact number.

Imagine, a loving God, a God who created the whole world sending 4 billion people into hell. What kind of God is that? It makes no sense. But you might say, according to Acts 4: 12, "There is no other name given under the sun by which man may be saved." But then again, in Luke 13: 29, Jesus says: "People will come from east and west and from north and south and will take their place in the Kingdom of God; the last will be first and the first will be last." Is it possible that Acts: 4:12 is more of a "confessional statement" made by an enthusiastic Peter who lived in the first century, who was unaware of other religions, rather than an objective, declarative statement normative for all ages and religions? You may want to think about that.

You might think that we are not supposed to use our common sense when it comes to matters of God and prayer and salvation. We have to take everything on faith. We may not understand everything clearly, but take it on faith. That is what a good Christian is supposed to do.
We have been doing that for centuries; we have been doing it all our lives. Look at the world around us. Is it a better place

because we have just taken everything on faith and never asked any questions? There is so much strife and war and aggression all around. There is so much greed and selfishness in this world. There is so much poverty and misery in this world. If we used our common sense, along with our faith, this world would be a much better place.

When Christians say "My God is bigger than your God," the Muslims say, "Christians are infidels." Both statements are nonsense, not common sense.

If you think about it, in most areas of life, except religion, we are using common sense. For example, if we need heart surgery, we don't call a medicine man like they did it in biblical times; we go the best hospital in town. If we need to travel to New York, we don't say, we need to travel on a donkey, because that is how people traveled in biblical times. Imagine traveling on a donkey on I-95. When we need to write something down, we don't look for papyrus parchment because that is what people in biblical times used for writing. We use computers, smart phones and iPads these days. **So what is it about religion that we are frozen in time, but in everything else we have come of age?**

I think the underlying reason is fear. We are afraid God will punish us. Because, in the Old Testament that is what God did most of the time. If you disobey God, you get fried. God will take you out even for just being curious. Look at the story in I Sam; 6: 19-20. The Ark of the Covenant was being taken through the city. It was like a parade; people gathered on the side of the street. The Ark was being carried through the city of Beth Shemesh and some of the men looked into the Ark of the Lord.

They just took a peek, purely out of curiosity. Do you know what happened to them? They were killed on the spot. I am not making this up. V. 19 says: "But God struck down some of the men of Beth Shemesh, putting 70 of them to death, because they had looked into the Ark of the Lord." Think of the wives and children of these 70 men suddenly becoming widows and orphans because their husbands looked into the Ark of the Covenant, the seat of God! V.20: "Seeing this, the men of Beth Shemesh asked: "Who can stand in the presence of the Lord, this holy God?"

The God of Jesus does not want us to be afraid; The God of Jesus will not smite us if we are curious about God. The God of Jesus will not punish us if we are confused about prayer and how salvation works. The God of Jesus wants us to grow up; the God of Jesus wants us to use the brain that God gave us for discernment; the God of Jesus wants us to believe that His spirit is embedded in our hearts. The God of Jesus wants us to ask questions. The God of Jesus wants us to use our God-given common sense; that is how you become mature disciples.

3. Undigested Faith
Mark 8:31-36

He then began to teach them that the Son of Man must suffer many things and be rejected by the elders, chief priests and teachers of the law, and that he must be killed and after three days rise again. He spoke plainly about this, and Peter took him aside and began to rebuke him. But when Jesus turned and looked at his disciples, he rebuked Peter. "Get behind me Satan!" he said. "You do not have in mind the things of God, but the things of men."

Then he called the crowd to him along with his disciples and said: "If anyone would come after me, he must deny himself and take up his cross and follow me. For whoever wants to save his life will lose it, but whoever loses his life for me and for the gospel will save it. What good is it for a man to gain the whole world, yet forfeit his soul?

Socrates once said that an unexamined life is not worth living. I think that Socrates is right on the money. What is an unexamined life? It is a life that has no purpose or goal. It is a life with no dreams. It is a life that takes everything on its face value, without asking any questions. It is a life that is lived following the norms of society, than your own ideas and meanings. In short, it is a life lived without awareness.

I feel that a lot of people are sleep-walking through life. You know what sleep-walking means. I have not done that, but I had patients who had that problem. They wake up in the middle of sleep and walk but they are not aware that they are doing it.

Many people sleep walk through life, because, they are not aware of what they are really doing each day of their lives or why they do what they do. Deepak Chopra calls it the "hypnosis of social conditioning." What it means is that we often follow the prevailing fads in society. Instead of thinking for ourselves, we go with the masses. That is why corporations buy commercials during Super Bowl paying up to three million dollars for a 30 seconds spot. They know they can hypnotize the masses, using mesmerizing colors and techniques. It works; otherwise they won't spend that kind of money. People can be so gullible.

People are so influenced by others that they vote against their own self interests. Case in point: One third of Texans don't have health insurance and almost 25% of children in that state have no coverage. Yet, almost 9 in 10 Texans opposed the health care bill, also known as *Obama Care,* because they were told by their leaders, for political reasons, that the bill was bad for them.

According to Neale Donald Walsch, "the world is in the condition it is in, because the world is full of sleepwalkers, living in a dream and watching that dream turn into a nightmare."

If sleep walking is true of life in general, it is truer of religious life for most people, because religion is part of social conditioning.

I don't know about you, but I did not choose my religion; I was born into it. I was born in a very traditional Catholic family. My parents were staunch Catholics. They attended Mass every Sunday. They baptized me when I was seven days old, because they believed that if a child died without baptism, he is headed for limbo, which by the way, Pope John Paul II removed from the list as a final destination for un-baptized infants.

I was told that good people go to church and good boys serve as altar boys. So I became an altar boy at the age of 10 and went to church, walking 3 miles, every Saturday and Sunday to serve Mass. In those days, Mass was said in a language called *Syriac*; it is a Persian language, a derivative of Hebrew, and I learned the prayers of the Mass in *Syriac* and repeated them without understanding them.

Every Sunday, we had catechism class before the Mass. I remember this teacher, a respected elder in the church, reading from the official catechism book of the Church. He was teaching us about the creation of the world. He said that God created heaven and earth and everything in it in six days and on the seventh day, God rested.

So I asked him, how does God take rest? Does God take a nap? What was God doing on the seventh day? The teacher's face turned red. He gave me this stern look and said: "He was creating hell for kids like you who ask such stupid questions."

He also told my parents that I was asking stupid questions in catechism class. Since then, for a long time, I never asked any questions. I just believed. I was taught that Jesus is both divine and human; I was taught that Mary was both virgin and mother; I was taught that Jesus came into this world to die for my sins; that Jesus is now sitting at the right hand of God, and will come again to judge the living and the dead at the end of world.

But I never grasped the meaning of these teachings that I was told to believe. And so it didn't make much of a difference in my life.

Frances Bacon once said, "It is not what we eat but what we digest that makes us strong; not what we gain but what we save that makes us rich; not what we read but what we remember that makes us learned; not what we preach but what we practice that makes us whole."

"It is not what we eat, but what we digest that makes us strong." Now think about that for a moment. You can put into your stomach all you can eat from a Chinese buffet, but if that food does not digest and become part of you, it will not nourish you.

This is very true of religion. Unless you grasp the meaning of what you believe, it won't do you any good. In my line of work as a hospice chaplain, I meet a lot of religious people who have not grasped the meaning of their religion; they have not digested what they have eaten from the religious buffet. And I see them suffer, especially, on and around death beds.

I visited a home last week. The patient was an 82 year old woman, Jane, who had COPD due to emphysema. She was born and raised Catholic. She had believed all the articles of Catholic faith and had repeated the Apostles' Creed many times. But none of that seemed to help her during her pain and suffering. She was angry and miserable. She was so upset that her three children don't visit her often. She was mad that her sister who lives in Ocala has not come to see her. She is so impatient and demanding that she makes Jim, her male friend, very frustrated and nervous. Jim was rolling his eyes and grumbling under his breath during the entire time of my visit.

I asked Jim if he wanted to talk or needed some help, and he said: "I don't do religion." He seemed miserable; but of course, he does not do religion.

But Jane did religion; she was a Catholic all her life. She told me: "I want to get out of this lousy world; I hate my life."

I felt so helpless; she had no awareness, no insight, and no peace. Jane was wearing a necklace with a crucifix. I held that crucifix in my hands and told her: "You are wearing a beautiful crucifix; what does that mean to you? "I don't know, I had it for years, I never thought much about it," she said.

Cross is Christianity's most important symbol. Crosses are found in most churches. In protestant churches, the cross is devoid of the broken body of Jesus, pointing to the resurrection. In Catholic churches, Jesus is on the cross, still bearing bloody wounds. But in whatever form, the cross symbolizes that the death and resurrection of Jesus are at the center of Christianity.

Lot of people wear a cross around their neck. Jane had one, too. But it didn't help her much in time of her dire need because, as she said: "I never thought much about it." It was like undigested food. It did not nourish her.

Cross is the ultimate symbol of suffering and death, not just any suffering and death, but undeserved suffering and death. Jesus was only 33 years old. He did not hurt anybody. He challenged people about their way of life, and they didn't like it, especially the religious authorities of his time, because he challenged the way they did religion. They wanted to get rid of him so that they could continue to do their religion.

Crucifixion is the most heinous and painful mode of capital punishment that humans have ever devised. Lethal injection that is used in the United States is a very humane way of killing people. There is no pain involved. Even guillotine, which the French used, killed its victims in less than a minute. Death by hanging is also instant, may be painful for a minute or two.

But crucifixion? Imagine somebody driving a nail into your palm. Try that with a pin. Try that on the arch of your foot...ouch. Imagine wearing a crown of thorns on your head. Imagine hanging with the entire weight of your body pulling down from the nails. Imagine hanging naked, exposed to the elements, jeered and ridiculed by the crowd... imagine dying rejected, dejected, abused and abandoned...even apparently by his own

Father. That is why Jesus cried out: *"Eloi Eloi.lama sabachthani…*My God, my God, why have you forsaken me?" (Mk.15:34)

So that is cross for you in a nutshell. If you wear that cross around your neck, it has to mean something to you. If you understand the meaning of that cross and clutch it with faith, all your pain and suffering should melt away, because nothing that you are going through can remotely resemble what Jesus went through. **That cross you wear around your neck is supposed to give you comfort in your moments of suffering, sadness, loneliness and abandonment.**

But it is more than just comfort. The cross is supposed to give you hope. Hope that this too will pass; whatever you may be going through, this too will pass, because it passed for Jesus. His suffering and pain, resulted in ultimate victory over death. He rose again, glorified and fully transformed to a new life. As disciples of Jesus, that is our hope that those who partake in the sufferings of Christ will also partake in his glory.

When I go through a rough moment in my life, be it some physical or emotional pain, anxiety, rejection or hopelessness, I clutch the cross around my neck, I close my eyes, and place my suffering and pain at the foot of the cross, and immediately my eyes well up with tears of release and my lips will silently say:

"Thank you Jesus." My pain becomes bearable, not merely from the memory of the sufferings of Jesus, but from the power that Jesus gives me to face my pain.

The cross of Jesus is packed with power, power to redeem us from the negative experiences of life and transform us and take us to a higher level.

So, take a moment to examine your belief system. Does what you believe impact your life? When the rubber meets the road, does it make a difference that you are a disciple? So, the question to ask is: "Am I unconsciously repeating the articles of faith for the sake of tradition or do they affect and change my life?

For example, reflect on these words of Jesus: "If anyone would come after me, he must deny himself, take up his cross and follow me." **If cross is the path of discipleship, we should not be surprised by any suffering that might come our way.**

4. I Don't Believe in God Anymore
Text: 1John 4: 16b-21

God is love. Whoever lives in love lives in God, and God in him. In this way, love is made complete among us so that we will have confidence on the Day of Judgment, because in this world we are like him. There is no fear in love. But perfect love drives out fear, because fear has to do with punishment. The one who fears is not made perfect in love. We love because he first loved us. If anyone says, "I love God," yet hates his brother, he is a liar. For anyone who does not love his brother, whom he has seen, cannot love God, whom he has not seen. And he has given us this command: Whoever loves God must also love his brother.

Once upon a time, a holy man sent his disciples to have a shirt made for a special occasion. "God be praised," said the tailor; "God willing, I will have it ready for you next week." When the disciples returned the next week, the shirt was not ready. Again, the tailor said: "God willing, I will deliver it in 3 days." Still, it was not completed and the tailor told the disciples: "God willing, I will surely finish it next week." A frustrated holy man, told his disciples: *"Ask him how long it will take to make the shirt, if he leaves God out of it?"*

We are all familiar with the "God-talkers." Being a hospice chaplain, I spent most of my day in religious circles. Excessive God-talk is jarring to my ears. There are people who preface everything they say with 'God' and my unscientific survey has revealed that the more they "talk" about God the less they "walk" with God, because I believe that "those who talk don't know and those who know don't talk."
Then there are the "God-agents." These are usually T.V. preachers, priests, ministers and elders who think and act like

they know who God is and as if they have a special access to the mind of God. They talk authoritatively about the will of God for an individual or a congregation, and the people in the audience believe them and send money to them to spread the "Word of God" to the millions who have not heard it. They are usually dismissive of the God experiences in cultures and religions other than Christianity. They are meticulous about rites, rubrics and rituals for fear of offending God.

I was born in a "godly" culture and raised in a "godly" home by parents who feared and worshipped God more than loved God. We went to Mass on Sundays because missing Sunday Mass would be a sin against God. We observed Lent and fasted on Fridays to please God. I became a priest and I was officially a "God-talker" and "God agent" for thirteen years of my life. I gave up that role in 1988. But my passion for God has only increased since then. As a result, I have stopped just believing in God anymore.

One day during a bible study, I blurted out that I did not believe in God any more. The group members were flabbergasted. They did not know what to make of such an "ungodly" statement from a supposedly "godly" person, who is a former priest, an elder in his current church and a hospice chaplain. I made such a shocking statement to impress upon them an idea that hopefully they will never forget.

First of all, I don't believe in a "God up there" any more. I don't believe that God is an old man with a long beard sitting in an imaginary thrown beyond the clouds, a Supreme Being who needs my praise and adoration.

Secondly, instead of just "believing" in God, I "experience" God. Before I explain that in detail, let me talk about what "belief" in God does for us: Nothing much. It does not change our lives; it does not make us happier; it does not make the world a better place because **belief in God for many is often an intellectual assent to a *dogma about God* rather than a life-changing immersion into the Ground of our being, who is God.**

For example, let us just take the case of our country. According to a Pew Research survey, 99 percent of Americans believe in God. Atheists or agnostics are just a mere one percent. As a nation, we spent 714 billion dollars for the military, but we won't spend 7 billion for education.

Believers in God will fight tooth and nail against any reduction in military spending; believers in God have no problem taking huge salaries for themselves, but refuse to pay a meager salary for their workers. Believers in God abort a million babies in this country every year. Twenty-five percent of married men cheat on their wives, but all of them believe in God. Believers in God have no problem owning guns and even killing someone if necessary. **So, belief in God does not necessarily mean that believers behave in a godly manner.**

Pastor Phelps who pickets funerals of gay soldiers is a believer. He believes in Jesus. He is a very angry believer. The venom of hate and prejudice coming out of his mouth is just unbelievable.

Pastor Terry Jones who threatened to burn the *Koran* in Gainesville, Florida, which prompted the killing of 17 UN workers in Afghanistan, is a believer too. He is burning the holy book of another religion by holding the holy book of his religion, which by the way says, "Love your enemies." What kind of screwed up belief is that?

Adolf Hitler, who incinerated 6 million Jews, believed in God.

The 19 highjackers, who boarded those planes on 9/11/2001 and blew up the Twin Towers, believed in God. As a matter of fact, they woke up at 4 a.m. that day, took a shower, spread their prayer mats on the floor of their hotel room and did their morning prayers. They prayed to God for the success of their mission: the mission to kill innocent people. While storming into the cockpit with murderous force, they were chanting: "*Allahu akbar*," which means "God is great."

Moamer Khadaffi was a believer in God. He was an observant Muslim; he prayed five times a day. But he also oppressed his people for 42 year and killed anyone who opposed him, like rats.

Albert Mugabe, the former dictator of Zimbabwe was a staunch believer. He had his own private chapel in his palace. But he oppressed the poor people of his nation for so many years.

I can go on and on with hundreds of examples of so called leaders and the led who are believers in God, but their belief rarely became manifested in their behavior.

I see this in my line of work as a hospice chaplain. During the first visit to a patient, we are required to complete a *Spiritual Assessment*. It is a way of understanding where the patient is in his or her relationship to God. One of the questions on this assessment tool is about their belief in God.

Almost everyone says YES to that question. "Of course I believe in God," they would say. I am thinking of this patient who is 85 years old. She is an orthodox Jew who attended temple every Friday and kept a kosher home. But she was miserable. She always complained about her aches and pains. She was so upset with her sister who is 87, and they are not even talking to each other anymore. She was afraid that her money would run out and she would end up in a nursing home.

She was mad at the staff at the ALF (Assisted Living Facility) because, they didn't respond promptly enough when she needed help. None of the staff liked her, because she was demanding and demeaning of them. Over all, she was a very miserable person, but she believed in God. Her belief did not seem to help her deal with the fears, anxieties and inevitable irritations of life.

What I am saying is that abstract belief in a distant God does not make any difference in the day to day lives of people. The world is full of believers, but the world is not better for that. Just watch cable TV and you will see the arguing, the fighting, the acrimony, and the hate among people who believe in God.

So, I don't ask anybody "do you believe in God" because it really means nothing. I ask a different question: "Do you experience God?" because if you experience God, you are likely to have a relationship with God which is likely to change your life. Belief is more abstract and experience, is more tangible.

Let me give you example as to how life changes when we graduate from the level of belief to the level of experience. I was in a Clinical Pastoral Education Program for six months. There were seven other chaplains in the group. We met once a week for five hours. It is an intense class with multidimensional learning through sharing lives, writing papers, peer counseling, supervisor sessions, etc. One of the participants was a southern Baptist minister. She was a traditional pastor for 30 years serving largely conservative churches in Louisiana.

When we started the program, she believed that homosexuality was a sin, because she was taught that sexuality is a choice. She did not exactly hate gays, but she did not like them either. She thought they were destined for hell. Now, she is in this group where one of the chaplains happens to be gay. He is a wonderful human being, talented, compassionate, and full of life. He has been in a monogamous relationship with his partner for 27 years. He is loved by his patients for the tender care he provides them and admired by his peers for his vivacious personality.

After sitting next to him in the same room for six months, talking to him and listening to him talk about his family, friends, and his life experiences, this Baptist minister became his best friend. She began calling him her brother. They forged a beautiful friendship. See how an abstract belief, a negative belief in this case, about gay people, turned into a close friendship and even admiration, after experiencing a gay person up close and personal.

This happens in all areas of our lives. Think of your neighborhood. There could be a neighbor whom you always see from far and does not even know his name. One day you take a chance to walk over to him, introduce yourself and talk to him. After that meeting, your opinion of that person changes; because now you have an experience of him, not just a mere belief about him.

This happened to me at work last week. There is a nurse who works in our company. I have passed in front of her office in the last four years, but never said hello, because she is always focused on her work and rarely looks up when people pass in front of her office. Two weeks ago, her son, who was only 27 years old, died. He was fighting cancer for many years. So I went for the funeral; stood in line and gave her a hug and offered my condolences. This was the first time I had spoken to this person in four years of working for the same company.

She returned to work last week. As usual, I passed in front of her office; and as usual she did not look up. I knocked on the door, went in, gave her a hug and talked to her. I have a totally new relationship with Nancy now, because of my experiences with her in the last few weeks.

Something similar has to happen for us in our relationship to God; it has to move from a mere belief in a supernatural deity to the level of a closeness and connection to a reality that is closer to us than we can ever imagine.

There are so many examples in the Bible about belief moving to experience which changes people's lives. Abraham had an experience with the angels of God, and that radically changed his life; Moses had an experience of God on Mount Sinai, and that changed him. Saul had an experience of the risen Lord and that changed him from Saul of Tarsus, the persecutor of Christians, to St. Paul, the greatest apostle to the Gentiles.

Zacheus, the hated tax collector who had merely heard about Jesus, had a personal experience of Jesus at his house and that completely changed his life. The Samaritan woman had an experience of Jesus that changed her life and the life of the entire Samaritan village that came to know Jesus through her.

All through the bible, we can see that it is experience not just belief that transforms life.

Let me give you an example from secular life. Belief is something like knowing that there are 13 trillion dollars in circulation in the country. Experience means how much of that trillion is in your bank account. Having all that money in the country means nothing to you, unless it is in your account. *Believing* that God is almighty and benevolent is not going to make much difference. *Experiencing* God as almighty and benevolent will make all the difference.

So how do you experience this God that you believe in? I think the first step in that process is to re-examine and possibly change the idea of God that you have in your head. Take a moment to think about it. When you hear the word GOD what image or thoughts come to your mind?

Most likely you thought about this Supreme Being who is separate from us, who is above us, who is watching over us, who demands our obedience and worship. A being who listens to our prayers, grants some requests and defers others, because it is not "good for us." I don't blame you for thinking like this, because, that is what the creed has taught us and we have repeated it for centuries: "I believe in God, the father almighty, creator of heaven and earth." It is an intellectual belief not an emotional experience. It is a God who is so far away; it is so hard to touch and feel and experience that God.

Instead of trying to experience God from the "top down," let us try from the "bottom up."

Look around the people in this church. What do you see? Remember, it is not what you *look* at what matters, it is what you *see*. Do you *see* them as images of God? Do you love them? I am sure you do, because you are surrounded by nice people. But use your imagination to look at the people in your neighborhood, the people in the mall, the drivers on the road, people of a different color, people who are gays; people who are Democrats, people who are Republicans; people of other countries, the Muslims, the Hindus, the Jews; do you *see* them as images of God? Do you love them?

When your mind is broad enough and heart is wide enough to include and love ALL people, you will start experiencing God because as John said: "Everyone who loves has been born of God and knows God. No one has ever seen God; but if we love one another, God lives in us and his love is made complete in us."

5. America's Four Gods
Text: John 1:14

The Word became flesh and dwelt among us. We have seen his glory, the glory of the One and only, who came from the Father, full of grace and truth.

I like to talk to you about a book that just came out last month. It has a fascinating title: *America's Four Gods*; but the sub-title is what got my attention the most: *What we say about God and what that says about us.*

So what we think about God, says a lot about us

It is a serious book, because it is not just the opinion of an author. It is based on the most comprehensive survey of America's religious beliefs, done by two researchers, Paul Froese and Christopher Bader, both professors of Sociology at Baylor University.

The book begins by posing a dilemma: *It is not very clear what Americans mean when they talk about God. Yet references to God are everywhere. A presidential speech always ends with "God bless America." The phrase is all over bumper stickers and bill boards. The Pledge of Allegiance reminds us that we are a "nation under God:" and the US currency assures us that "in God we trust."*

More than one hundred years ago, German philosopher Fred Nietzsche declared that "God is dead." But despite living in the most modernized and technologically advanced country, Americans report one of the world's highest levels of belief in God.

The strange thing is that even though we say we believe in God, we avoid deep discussions about God. That is why we are advised not to discuss politics or religion in polite company.

The authors found that 99 percent of Americans believe in God. About one percent of the population is atheists. So there is great consensus there. So the rift is not between believers and atheists, or those of different faiths; what divides us is what we *think* of God and the role God plays in our daily lives.

Based on their findings, the authors place believers in America into four broad groups: Believers in an Authoritative God, Benevolent God, Critical God and Distant God (ABCD). When I explain each group, try to see which God you believe in.

The first group, 31 per cent, believe in an *Authoritative God*. Believers in an Authoritative God are most likely to imagine God as a literal father, humanlike, male and commanding in appearance. Believers in an Authoritative God are convinced that Gd judges human behavior. They feel that God can become very angry and is capable of meting out punishment to those who are unfaithful or ungodly. When Pat Robertson said that Hurricane Katrina was a punishment from God on New Orleans for their partying and other excesses, he was referring to this God.

The second group, 24 per cent, believe in a *Benevolent God*. Members of this group are less likely to think that God judges and punishes human behavior. Instead the Benevolent God is mainly a force for good in the world and is less willing to condemn individuals. Believers in a benevolent God are usually happy, upbeat and positive.

The third image of God, the *Critical God*, is believed by 16 per cent of the population. The Critical God is different from the Authoritative God, in that the Critical God punishes people without engaging with the people. Believers feel that God's judgment will be felt, if not now, definitely in the next life and punishment in hell. For example Pope Benedict XI is very adamant about this issue. He said: "Hell exists and is eternal, even if nobody talks about it much anymore." What the pope is saying is that God may be slow to act now, but He is going to get you later!

The fourth image of God, the *Distant God*, is believed by 24 per cent; they view God as a cosmic force that sets the laws of nature in motion but does not really do things in the world or hold clear opinions about our activities or world events. They refuse to assign a gender to God like a "He" or a "She." In addition, a distant God does not require offering and praise and does not respond to our prayers and requests.

So, there you have it, America's four gods, the Authoritative God, the Benevolent God, the Critical God, and the Distant God; It is easy to remember as ABCD.

So what is your image of God? Do you belong to any of the four groups or do you have your own image? It is a good idea to think about it and articulate your ideas about God, because your image of God says a lot about you. According to sociologist Andrew Greely, "God is the foundation of our world view." How we view God determines how we see the world and behave in the world.

For example a person who pickets abortion clinics and shows up at the funerals of gay soldiers is more likely to believe in a critical God; a person who does not attend churches or say any prayers is likely to believe in a distant God; or a person who thinks that the whole world is a hostile place and there is evil lurking at every corner, is more likely to believe in an authoritative God. As we can see, God is a very controversial topic. The authors of this book divide the population into four broad categories and there are numerous distinctions within that group. If you check out the website, *God.com*, you will see millions of images of God.

If I were to choose an image of God proposed by this book, I would choose God as benevolent. I don't think God punishes anybody; any punishment we feel is the result of the choices we make as individuals or as a group. The God that Jesus portrays in the Gospel is always a loving father.

I like to share with you another image of God that is the foundation of my spiritual life. It is the image of God that we celebrate during the Christmas season. We think that Christmas is about Christmas trees, Christmas parties, and Christmas presents. None of these have anything really to do with Christmas; they are all peripheral to Christmas.

The event of Christmas is about an image of God. It is about God becoming Man; Christmas is about God's image as a human being. Almighty God became a human being. Apostle Paul says: "Though he was in the form of God, he did not deem equality with God something to be grasped at. Rather, he emptied himself and took the form of a slave, being born in the likeness of men." (Phil.2:6-8)

So if God chose to take the human form, there has to be something special about the human form. What God is saying is that humanity is important; human beings are special. **If you are looking for the invisible God, don't go about searching far away heavens, but look around you, and look at the visible, tangible human being standing right in front of you. That human being is God's incarnation. That human being is a representative of God who became man, today.**

To me that is the real meaning of Christmas. I get very little inspiration from looking at a plastic Jesus in a crib and thinking about Christmas; I don't want to celebrate Christmas by gazing lovingly at a ceramic Jesus in a manger scene and commenting to others how cute baby Jesus looks. **It is so easy to see baby Jesus in a lifeless ceramic figurine; but it is so challenging to see**

Jesus in the living human being standing next you.

Think of all the people in your life: family, friends, neighbors, and the people of the world at large. You may love some, dislike a few, and discard the millions as irrelevant to your life. **You cannot celebrate Christmas, the event of God becoming man, by disliking, discarding, and dishonoring human beings.**

Do you know why Christmas comes and goes every year, and nothing serious happens to us spiritually? Because we have not understood or celebrated the deeper meaning of Christmas, as honoring the divinity of humanity.

"How can you love God, whom you cannot see, if you cannot love man whom you can see?" asks Apostle John.

So that is the challenge of Christmas. I think if you try it, it becomes easier each day. **First of all, you have to believe that all human beings, regardless of their religious or sexual orientation, or any other labels you want to place on them, are potential extensions of Jesus.**

I don't deny the fact there are evil people in the world, doing bad things. But by and large, I believe that humans are basically good; every person is an image of God; every person is Jesus in human form.

I had a great experience of that when we were flying back from India. We landed in Kuwait airport at 7 a.m. in the morning. Our next flight to New York was at 10 a.m. So we went to a corner of the airport with very little traffic. There were plenty of couches to lie down and stretch. We were next to Gate number one. There was an officer checking passengers, patting them down before the flight. That flight was going to Istanbul, Turkey. The plane left, he locked the gate and came to us and began talking to us. He was extremely friendly.

After exchanging pleasantries, he walked away. Ten minutes later, he comes with a full tray of food and drinks: Four paper bags of food, and four big cups of Pepsi. I was a bit suspicious. What is this stranger trying to do? He was obviously a Muslim. My wife is a Caucasian and American. Did he put something in the food? I was hesitant to eat it. But the kids, hungry and obviously innocent, began to eat. My wife began to sip the Pepsi. She said that we have to have faith in humanity. I didn't eat; I said to myself: "At least one of us had to be healthy!"

An hour before our flight, the man comes back. He takes us to the front of the line where hundreds of passengers were waiting in line to be screened. He takes us first, and lets us go through the security gate without even patting us down. Other passengers standing in line gave us funny looks. The man took us straight to the first four seats in the waiting lounge. And he gave us four cans of orange juice to drink.

After checking all the passengers, he came back and talked to us some more; He wanted to take a picture with my family. He gave me his phone number and told me to call him when I was in Kuwait the next time. His name was Gillis Hameed. To me, it was a great Christmas experience; looking back, I believe that Gillis Hameed was Jesus.

Every person you see out there may not look like the image of Jesus you are familiar with, or behave like Jesus. But you have to keep looking. Look beyond what you see on the outside. Every time you look at a human being, think of God becoming man. That is how you celebrate Christmas by finding the God who took the human form. And what you find out there in the world, largely depends on who *you* are.

6. From EGO to FROG
Text: Matthew 6: 25-34

Therefore I tell you, do not worry about your life, what you will eat or drink; or about your body, what you will wear. Is not life more important than food, and the body more important than clothes? Look at the birds of the air; they do not saw or reap or store away in barns, and yet your heavenly father feeds them. Are you not much more valuable than they? Who of you by worrying can add a single hour to his life?

And why do you worry about clothes? See how the lilies of the field grow. They do not labor or spin. Yet I tell you that not even Solomon in all his splendor was dressed like one of these. If that is how God clothes the grass of the field, which is here today and tomorrow is thrown into the fire, will he not much more clothe you, O you of little faith? So, do not worry, saying, 'What shall we eat' or 'What shall we drink?' or 'What shall we wear?' For the pagans run after all these things, and your heavenly Father knows that you need them, but seek first his kingdom and his righteousness, and all these things will be given to you as well.

When hurricane Wilma hit in 2005, a church in North Florida was destroyed. They lost everything and the congregation gathered in a school auditorium for worship. The pastor told them that this was the time to be FROGs: Fully Rely On God. A lady in the church got an idea. She made green plastic frogs, attached a note "Fully Rely On God," and sent them to her friends. It grew to thousands.

Many people would say that they fully trust or rely on God, but when push comes to shove, it doesn't seem that way. I see this in my hospice ministry all the time. Many patients, who are approaching death, are often confused and scared. They are worried about leaving their loved ones; they are anxious about death itself, and many are afraid that God would punish them. All the faith and trust they thought they had is not helping them at this critical juncture in their life.

I am reminded of a story of a man who was very proud of his faith in God. "I put my complete trust in God my savior" he used to say. So one day, God decided to test him. The man fell into a deep ravine. Before reaching the ground, he got hold of the branch of a tree, and he was hanging there. You can only hang for a few minutes at best like that. So he began praying to God whom he totally trusted.

Then he heard a voice from the top. "Do you trust me?" and the man said, "I do; I have always trusted you; you are my God, where can I go from you; please save me."

Then the voice said: "If you trust me totally and believe in your heart that I can save you, let go of the branch." The man looked down; he knew how the law of gravity works; he knew he would surely die from the fall. He thought for a moment, and asked: "Is there anyone else up there?"

The so called trust in God that many people talk about is very often like that. When the room gets crowded, trust leaves through the back door. When the rubber meets the road, trust doesn't apply. So, how do we become FROGs or fully rely on God? First, let me make two observations about how not to go about fully relying on God.

Fully relying on God does not mean being naive or foolish. Let me tell you a story. Once upon a time, there was a man who fully trusted God. There was a huge flood in his home town. As the water rose around his house, his neighbors packed up and went to emergency shelters. He refused. He stayed back saying that God would save him as Noah was saved from the flood. The man knew his Bible. As the water rose, he climbed on the roof of his house. Then a rescue boat came by and asked him to jump in so that they could take him to safe ground.

He refused again saying that his God whom he trusted totally would save him. Few minutes later, a helicopter came by, lowered its rope ladder and asked the man to climb up. He refused again trusting that God would save him. Finally, the water rose more and he drowned. When he reached heaven, he was furious with God. "I trusted you fully and you let me die" and God said: "I sent a boat and a helicopter to save you, what else do you want from me?"

The second point I want to make is actually related to the first. Who is this God that you put your trust in? Think about that for a moment. More than likely, you are thinking about this Almighty Being who is bigger and greater than you in size, power, and might, who controls everything in our lives. It is a *He*, of course. He listens to our prayers and answers them. Sometimes, it feels like He doesn't listen to our prayers. Then we find excuses such as "it may not be good for me at this time" or "God's ways are not man's ways" etc.

If such an idea of God works for you, by all means, keep it. But from my experience in meeting with a lot of people at their death beds, trust in such a distant God rarely works when they most need it. They are still afraid, anxious, and unforgiving, and die with uncertainty and fear.

But there is a better way. At least, a way that works for me. I trust in a God who is so much part of me that even if I wanted to get away from that God, I cannot. It is the God who David talks about in Psalms 139:

Where can I go from your Spirit? Where can I flee from your presence? If I go up to the havens, you are there; if I make my bed in the depths, you are there; O Lord, you have searched me and you know me; you discern my going out and my lying down.

Then there is this powerful verse: *You created my inmost being; you knit me together in my mother's womb, I praise you because I am fearfully and wonderfully made.*

Prophet Jeremiah echoes the same sentiment when he talks about how deeply and personally God knows him: *Before I formed you in your mother's womb, I knew you. (Jer.1:5)*

This God is the ground of my being. Paul talks about this God in the *Acts of the Apostles* as he was visiting the gentiles in Athens. He told them: *The God who made the world and everything in it, the Lord of heaven and earth does not live in temples built by hands...This God is not far from any one of us; for in him we live, move and have our being. (Acts 17:28)*

Why do I totally trust this very *Ground of my being*? I turn my imagination towards my beginnings: The beginning of my life. I want you to join me in this fantasy tour; you can do it with you as the main character.

I am 5'6" tall and weigh 167 pounds. There are about 75 trillion cells in my body. That is 75,000,000,000,000, with 12 zeroes!

But I started out as a zygote with a single cell, in a remote village in southern India. When I started, I was just one cell and each day, it multiplied exponentially and through an amazing process of miraculous metamorphosis and meticulous manufacturing, I began to grow in my mother's womb. As weeks and months went by, I began to take shape. In the beginning I was just an undifferentiated mass of flesh. Hands and legs had no fingers; they were just stumps. Eyes had no lids; heart had no chambers.

Inside my mother's womb, God was at work. He made sure

that I had a heart and it had four chambers; God made sure that the arteries and veins were properly attached. Then came the biggest project; the digestive system. It is four times longer than my height. Our digestive system is about 24 feet long; but it stays so nicely tucked inside of us.

The mystery of my evolution in my mother's womb is that neither of my parents had to remember to do anything else after that night they came together. It is not like three months into her pregnancy, my mom said: "Today is the day the baby's lungs are made, I need to breathe harder" or six months into her pregnancy, my dad said: "Today, he is going to get his legs; let me make sure he has two of them." No involvement, participation or planning; it all just happened with so much beauty and precision.

Think about the first nine months of your life in your mother's womb. Do you remember worrying if God is going to give you one leg or two legs? Do you ever remember swimming in the amniotic fluid and wondering if God would remember to attach ten fingers to your hands? Were you anxious that God would remember to close your belly button and open your mouth at birth? Do you remember saying to yourself: "I hope my lungs that are flat like pancakes will open up like balloons when I come out."

You didn't worry about any of that; you didn't become anxious about any of that. God, the *Creative Force,* the *Ground of your being,* the *Alpha and the Omega,* took care of the entire process. And you came out into this world perfectly beautiful. God was totally in charge; you fully relied on Him during that time.

As a matter of fact, your dependence of parents continued for many more years after birth. They took care of you and provided for you. I don't ever remember, as an infant, lying awake at night, being worried and anxious about anything. If I was awake at that age, most probably I had colic, but not anxiety.

So what happened? What happened to that total reliance on God that took us flawlessly through the initial years? We grew up. We became adults; we began to become anxious and worried, untrusting, suspicious, guilty and depressed, angry and jealous, and aggressive and revengeful. Reliance on God went out through the window, and ego took over. We became the master of our own destiny. We took charge of our lives. And look where it takes us!

EGO stands for Edging God Out. So today, I invite you to think about your original state as zygotes, fetuses, embryos and children. Jesus said: "Unless you become like little children, you will not enter the kingdom of heaven." He was not talking about going to heaven after we die; he was talking about experiencing the peace, joy, and tranquility of heaven now, by being childlike in our attitude to life.

So, I am fully relying on God not because of promises pending, but because of promises kept. I am not looking to the future with anxiety; I am looking at the past with gratitude. I am not looking at the 75 trillion cells that I am today and worrying if some of them would divide fast and become cancerous, but I am thinking of the single cell that I was, and how marvelously it turned out.

The reason why we get so bent out of shape in life is that we are always living in the future. We are worried about what is going to happen tomorrow. We are not paying attention to what is happening today. We easily forget what God did for us in the past. When I think about it, God has done plenty, and I have no reason to think that it is going to change now or in the future.

I rely on God, not because of promises pending; but because of promises kept.

When you feel like being sad or anxious or worried, remember these words of Jesus: "Do not let your hearts be troubled; trust in God. Trust also in me."(Jn.14:1)

7. Does God Control Traffic Signals?
Text: 1King 19: 9-13

And the word of the Lord came to him: "What are you doing here, Elijah?" He replied, "I have been very zealous for the Lord God Almighty. The Israelites have rejected your covenant, broken down your altars, and put your prophets to death with the sword. I am the only one left, and now, they are trying to kill me too."

The Lord said, "go out and stand on the mountain in the presence of the Lord, for the Lord is about to pass by."

Then a great and powerful wind tore the mountains apart and shattered the rocks before the Lord, but the Lord was not in the wind. After the wind there was an earthquake, but the Lord was not in the earthquake. After the earthquake came a fire, but the Lord was not in the fire. And after the fire came a gentle whisper. When Elijah heard it, he pulled his cloak over his face and went out and stood at the mouth of the cave. Then a voice said to him, "What are you doing here, Elijah?"

Some of you know that I had knee surgery last month. Ten days after my surgery, I had to drive to Faith Christian Church in Hollywood. There was a heavy wrap around my knee and bending it was uncomfortable. Applying the break was the hardest. So I prayed for green lights. I wished I could put the car on cruise control and drive non-stop. It is impossible to do that on a busy street like University Drive. There are 37 traffic signals between Riverside Drive and Stirling Road, and stopping at even half of them would stress my knee. So I prayed for continuous green lights. I put my car on cruise control at 48 miles an hour.

After passing Southgate Blvd., I was excited because the next two lights were green. I said to myself, I will have to stop at McNab Rd, but I went through. Commercial Blvd is a big intersection.

"There is no way I will go through that without stopping" I said to myself. But I went through that again and I passed through the next several intersections without stopping. The first time I had to stop was at Broward Blvd. An 8 mile stretch of continuous driving through 20 green lights!

It had never happened in my 22 years of driving on University Drive. It was a miracle!

So when I went home, I posted on face book: *When you are in harmony with the Universe and peace with humanity, all your prayers will be answered.*

Next day, I got a comment from one of my Facebook friends, who is a city planner. He wrote: "Paul, the Lord works in mysterious ways; this month University Drive was one of the first two streets to get its signals synchronized, because you needed it now." And he sent me a link to the county website which had the following post:

Broward County is improving traffic flow through our "Green Lights Program," to coordinate traffic signals along our major streets. We will be re-timing our most frequently traveled roadways over the next several months according to the Green Lights Program schedule. Drivers traveling along streets where signal re-timing is in effect will experience fewer delays and more green lights."

They just started the program last month, and University Drive was one of the first 2 streets to get the benefit. I had the surgery last month. I needed an easy drive that Sunday and God blessed me with it; God blessed me through the efforts of the people at the traffic division. This is how my God works.

But another comment I received on my Facebook page said that I was trivializing God by dragging him down to the level of a traffic controller. The assumption behind that comment is that God is this Powerful Deity and we should not be associating him with mundane stuff like driving or eating or doing laundry.

I don't blame people for thinking like that because when you hear the word God, you are thinking of a Supreme Being. The predominant emotions associated with God are fear and respect, mystery and majesty. That is the image of God we see in the Bible, especially in the Old Testament. If you read the book of Exodus, the God you meet there is a powerful and frightening figure. It is a God who refuses to give his name to Moses. It is a God who denies Moses an opportunity to see His face. Seeing God face to face meant death.

According to Exodus 33: 21, the Lord said to Moses: *There is a place near me where you may stand on a rock. When my glory passes by, I will put you in a cleft in the rock and cover you with my hand until I have passed by. Then, I will remove my hand and you will see my back; but my face must not be seen.*

So the God of the Old Testament is so terrifying and glorious that Moses is only worthy to see his behind. I have no idea what God's behind looks like, then again I have no idea what His front looks like either.

My Facebook friend thinks that this Almighty God has no time or patience to be involved in the mundane job of giving me green lights on a city street. He is not the only one; according to a recent survey, 34% of Americans think that God is a distant figure. Benjamin Franklin said: "A supremely perfect God doesn't care one bit for such an inconsiderable nothing as man."

The fact is that there are many images for the same God; you can experience God in many ways. It is not a question of a right image or a wrong image, but the image that makes sense to you. You don't have to buy into the portrait of God you find in the

Book of Exodus, a frightening and intimidating deity who is distant from you; that is how the Israelites experienced God. You don't have to buy into Benjamin Franklin's idea of God, just because he is a great man. You have to experience God for yourself.

I experience God as intimately involved in ALL areas of my life, the trivial and the mundane, the ordinary, the boring and the routine aspects of my life and that of course includes driving my car on a busy city street and experiencing God as continuous green lights. That is what Apostle Paul meant when he told the people of Athens: "God is not far from any of us; in him we live and move and have our being." Separating us from God is like separating a fish from the water.

Psalm 139 beautifully explains how personally and deeply God is involved in the minutest details of our lives: *O Lord, you have searched me and found me. You know when I sit and when I rise; you perceive my thoughts from afar; You discern my going out and my lying down; you are familiar with all my ways; before a word is on my tongue, you know it completely."*

We are surrounded by God. There is no place we can go away from God's reach**.** *Where can I go from your spirit? Where can I flee from your presence? If I go up to the heavens, you are there; if I make my bed in the depths, you are there. If I rise on the wings of dawn, if I settle on the far side of the seas, even there, your hand will guide me, your right hand will hold me.*

Then comes the most powerful and the reassuring words of this Psalm, the rationale behind God's all pervasive presence and involvement in our lives. *For you created my inmost being; you knit me together in my mother's womb. I praise you because I am fearfully and wonderfully made (v.13).*

You knit me together in my mother's womb. I can never repeat those words without getting a chill. It shows how closely and intimately God is involved in the very delicate process of my beginnings in my mother's womb. Why would I think that such a God would abandon me to my devises once I am outside the womb?

And then the psalmist concludes with these beautiful words: *My frame was not hidden from you when I was made in the secret place. When I was woven together in the depths of the earth, your eyes saw my unformed body. All the days ordained for me were written in your book before one of them came to be!*

So our entire life, from the moment of conception till the last day on this earth, is book-ended by God; and this God is deeply involved in everything that happens to us and intimately present to everything we do. **We are held tenderly in the safety and security of this bubble, surrounded, supported and sustained by the Universe, like a fish in the water.**

By the way, *Universe* could be another name for God.

I encourage you to look for this God in the most ordinary and mundane aspects of your life. Today's reading encourages us to do that. Pay close attention to how the Lord appears to Elijah.

Prophet Elijah was in a pickle. The people had abandoned God and they were going to kill Elijah. So he wanted to meet and talk with his Lord God Almighty! The Lord told him to go and stand on the mountain to see the Lord.

Then three huge events happened. First, there was this powerful wind that tore the mountains apart and shattered the rocks, but the Lord was not in the wind.

After the wind, there was this humongous earthquake, but the Lord was not in the earthquake.

After the earthquake came this blazing fire but the Lord was not in the fire either.

After the fire came a gentle whisper, some translations say, a gentle breeze. *And the Lord was in the gentle breeze.*

So stop looking for God in the majestic and the miraculous. And start looking for God in the so called ordinary and the trivial, such as eating, driving, shopping, doing laundry and the gentle breeze all around you.

You will experience God in everything and everywhere, if you slow down and pay attention. "Be still and know that I am God."

All things reveal God; all experiences are epiphanies for those who have eyes to see. Elizabeth Barret Browning reminds us that there is a burning bush around every corner. "Earth is crammed with heaven and every common bush, afire with God; but only he who *sees*, takes off his shoes; the rest sit around and pluck blackberries."

When she wrote it years ago, she was referring to blackberry, the fruit. Today, people are so busy on their blackberries, iPhones, and iPods, that they fail to see God in ordinary experiences.

So, you can go through traffic lights worrying about your problems and getting angry with fellow drivers, or you can drive through them, being conscious of the pervasive presence and providence of God and thanking God for green lights.

8. Taking the Bible Seriously...Not Literally
Text: Deuteronomy 22:22-24

If a man is found sleeping with another man's wife, both the man and the woman must die. You must purge the evil from Israel. If a man happens to meet in a town a virgin pledged to be married and he sleeps with her, you shall take both of them to the gate of that town and stone them to death—the girl because she was in a town and did not scream for help, and the man because he violated another man's wife. You must purge the evil from among you.

Two weeks ago, on Saturday, the world was supposed to end. May 21st was supposed to have been *Judgment Day.* It was predicted by an 89 year old preacher by the name of Harold Camping in California. Camping is the founder of *Family Radio* in Oakland, heard in 48 different languages around the globe.

Camping told a TV reporter that when the world ends, "there's going to be big earthquakes that will make the one in Japan seem like a Sunday school picnic."

This isn't Camping's first prediction of the end of the world. He had previously predicted the date of Doomsday as being Sept. 6, 1994. The date came and went without the *Rapture* happening and without the *Tribulation* descending upon the Earth.

When nothing happened, he explained it as an error in his math, but this time he says it'll be different.

He said: "This day, May 21, 2011, is extremely important, as it will also be the first Day of Judgment, a time of horrible death and destruction, for all those left behind." Apparently the 'Elect' will be caught up in the Rapture on Saturday, leaving the rest of us sinners to face the music.

He said that there will be a five-month period for non-believers to get on board, because the real end will come on October 21st. So, Camping is kind enough to give the Chinese and the Hindus five months time to believe in Jesus so that they could be saved.

Camping apparently did not draw the date out of his hat or from thin air, but rather has developed actual math to support it.

According to paper reports, He believes that Christ was crucified on April 1, 33 A.D., exactly 722,500 days before May 21, 2011. That number, 722,500, is the square of 5 x 10 x 17. In Camping's numerological system, 5 represents atonement, 10 means completeness, and seventeen means heaven.

When the world did not end as he had predicted this time he said he missed the date by five months. So it is going to be on Oct 21st.

It is true that anybody with half a brain did not believe this nonsense; but millions did. There was a story about a retired transit worker in New York who spent his entire retirement savings of 140,000 dollars to print leaflets about the *Judgment Day* and distributed them to passengers on New York Subway. When he was interviewed on Sunday morning, he was so shaken. He did not know what to say, except clutch tightly to his Bible and babble about the math being wrong and that the end was going to be on Oct. 21st.
It created fear in the minds of children. A nurse who works with me has a 13 year old son, Michael. She shielded him from the news about the end of the world but Michael went to his friend's house on Friday night to play, and his friend's grandfather was watching TV. The news about the end of the world came on. Michael came home crying that night. He was afraid that the world was going to end the following morning. His main concern was that he would not get to watch the *Miami Heat* basket ball

game the next day.

According Harold Camping, parents had to prepare the children for the end of the world by telling them the truths of about God. Imagine tucking in little children Friday night using these words: "Mommy love you honey, sweet dreams, you are going to die tomorrow." Nice message to tell children right? And this guy is the founder of *Family Radio*, and telling your child that he is going to die is a family value?

Mr. Camping collected more than 100 million dollars from believers to spread his nonsense. He placed 2000 billboards across the nation. He also took out full page ads in major newspapers like, *The USA Today* and *the Wall Street Journal*, to spread his message. "Judgment day begins with a worldwide earthquake on May 21, 2011. Today is the day of salvation; cry unto God for mercy."

And, in this ad, he has quoted no less than a dozen Bible verses from the book of Daniel, Psalms, Jonah, Amos, Mathew, Mark, and 1st Corinthians. If you read them, you will find that these Bible verses are so unrelated to each other and the commentary is so erratic that you won't know what he is trying to say. For example, try this one: "The Bible declares that 'no man knows' is describing the unsaved condition of mankind. If you are saved then we may know all this spiritually discerned in God's word."

I read them carefully and became very confused. I have studied the Bible for 25 years. Imagine the kind of confusion and fear it can create in the minds of people who have no background in theology or biblical studies, which is 99 percent of Christians.

The saddest part of the story is that, according to Camping, the whole thing is 'Bible based.' And that is where I like to focus my reflection this morning. He says in the ad: "A multitude of faithful Bible students, that no man can number, agree: the end of this world, beginning on May 21, 2011, is established by God's Word, the holy Bible and God will shortly bring it to pass."

The 89 year old Camping said that his fifty yearlong study of the Bible is behind his claim. He said to a reporter: "I have no doubt at all, because I trust implicitly. I don't trust me or any man, but I trust the Bible implicitly."

My first reaction is that if this is what he could come up with after 50 long years of studying the Bible, he wasted his time. Here is a man who took the Bible literally, believing every word as it is written. Actually, he did not believe the entire Bible; he took words from just one book of the Bible, the book of *Revelations* and twisted its words to suit his purposes. It is in that book the author talks about the Second Coming of Christ. But the word *rapture* is not even mentioned in that book.

I have met a lot of people who say that they take the bible literally. Those who say that they take the Bible literally have not read the entire bible, because if they had read the whole book, they could not take it literally.

For example, according to Deut. 21: 18, "If a child disobeys his parents, he should be taken to the city gate, and be stoned to death." If our parents had literally followed that biblical injunction, how many of us would be sitting here? According to Lev. 20: 10, "If a man commits adultery with another man's wife, both of them should be put to death." It is funny that in the New Testament, they changed that rule. Because in the story of the woman caught in adultery in John 3, only the woman is brought before Jesus for stoning. The man gets a pass. They changed the biblical rule to favor man.

According to Deut. 22: 13, "If a husband finds out that his bride is not a virgin on the wedding night, she should be stoned to death." It is so shocking, but it is true; it is in the bible. If the husband reports to the father of the bride that she was not a virgin, the parents of the bride have to go to the elders of the town and prove to them that their daughter was a virgin. I don't know how you can prove it, but according to the bible, the father of the bride had to say: "Here is the proof of my daughter's virginity." (Deut. 22:17)

Then her parents shall display the cloth before the elders of the town and the husband will be punished with a fine of 100 shekels and given to the bride's father. If however, the charge is true, and no proof of the girl's virginity can be found, she shall be brought to the door of her father's house, and there, the men of her town shall stone her to death.

If we took these bible verses literally, how many brides will be killed in this country every weekend?

According to Exodus 22: 19, "Non-believers must be put to death." If we take that verse literally, we have to kill majority of the populations of China, India, Indonesia, and most of the Middle East.

Let me give you one more example. According to Exodus 31:16, "Whoever does any work on the Sabbath day must be put to death." If you take that bible verse literally, on Sundays, mass murder would take place in all the shopping malls, car dealerships, and hospitals in this country.

Mathew 5: 29 says: "If your right eye causes you to sin, gouge it out and throw it away." If you follow that literally, half of the world would be blind.

Those who claim to take the bible literally don't know what the bible really is or what it contains.

The word 'bible' comes from the Greek word *biblos*, meaning *book* the plural is *biblios* which means books. English words like *bibliography* and *library* come from this word. So, 'bible' just means a "collection of books." As a matter of fact, some of them are not even "books" in the traditional sense, because they are just one or two pages long. For example, *Philemon, 2 John, 3 John* and *Jude* are just one page each!

We should never forget that. We usually think of bible as just one book. But if you ask a Catholic, it is a collection of 72 books, but for Protestants, there are only 66 books. So, right there, we have a problem. The Catholics think that 72 books are inspired by God, while the Protestants would say, "Oh, no, God inspired only 66 books." The 72 books were chosen by the Catholic bishops who met during four Ecumenical Councils in Rome (382 AD), Hippo (393 AD) and both Councils of Carthage (397 & 419 AD). So, the first bible was put together in 420 AD.

In the 16th century, during the Protestant Reformation, Martin Luther moved 7 books of the Old Testament to an appendix at the end of bible. He wanted to get rid of several books of the New Testament such as *James, Hebrews, Jude* and *Revelations* but was talked into putting them back in.

In the 19th century, Protestant bibles dropped 7 books from the Old Testament completely.

If we cannot agree on the number of books in the bible, how can we agree on the message? Obviously we don't agree on the interpretations, and that is why there are 36,000 Christian denominations in the world; that is about 36,000 different interpretations of the 72/66 books.

It is very confusing and overwhelming for people who are busy with work, raising a family, putting food on the table etc. So, they blindly believe false prophets like Harold Camping.

So this is my advice for you: Please study the bible seriously; but don't just take every word you read literally. Ask questions. The sign of mature discipleship is the ability to ask questions in matters of faith and come to a *faith seeking understanding.* If you have no time to study the entire bible, read the Gospels, get to know the Jesus you meet on those pages. And don't just believe everything Church leaders and TV preachers say. Think for yourself, and try to see everything through the eyes of Jesus.

The irony is that Harold Camping's ad containing thousands of words, never mentions the name of Jesus. And the truth is that his full page ad has nothing to do with Jesus of Nazareth.

9. Think Different
Text: Mark 1: 14-16

After John was put in prison, Jesus went into Galilee, proclaiming the good news of God. "The time has come," he said. "The kingdom of God is near. Repent and believe in the good news!"

Repent is one of the first words out of the mouth of Jesus. According to Mt. 3:2, it is THE FIRST word that John the Baptist uttered. You hear this word repeatedly during the season of Lent. "Repent" is perhaps the most misunderstood word in the Bible today.

Many people think it means "feeling sorry for sins" or "turning from sin." That is not the biblical meaning of repentance. To understand its real meaning, we have to look up the meaning of the Greek word which is the original language of the bible. In the New Testament, the Greek word that we translate as "repent" is a compound word: *Meta-noeo.*

Meta means different, and *noeo* means thinking. *Noeo* is derived from *nous* which means mind. So, *metanoeo* means to "change your mind," or "change your thinking." Change your thinking in such a way that you will change your behavior.

Repentance traditionally understood as "feeling sorry for your sins or bad behavior," does not really change anything.

Take, for example, the case of domestic violence. A husband beats up his wife and the next day he feels so bad about it, apologizes and brings her flowers. Two weeks later, he beats her again and then repeats the same pattern. In domestic violence it is called the "cycle of abuse." Unless he goes into therapy and finds out the root cause of his abusive behavior by engaging his mind, he will never stop the behavior.

This is true of repentance in religion too. People commit sins; they feel sorry; they ask forgiveness; and they go and sin again. During my 13 years as a priest, I have heard thousands of confessions. Ninety nine percent of confessions are the same list of sins by the same people, almost repeated in the same order, month after month, year after year. Nothing really changes in their lives.

That is why today, I like to explain the biblical meaning of repentance as "change of mind." Jesus said: "Repent and believe in the good news." There is no mention of sin there. What he is saying is, change your mind about what you have been thinking so far about life, and start believing in the good news about the Kingdom of God. The Kingdom is not a faraway place, as you may have thought before, but it is right here, in the midst of you. The values of the Kingdom are very different from the values of the world. To know that, you have to change your thinking about a lot of things.

So, Repentance is the act of changing your thinking or having a different mind than the one you are having now. Changing your mind can change your outlook and changing your outlook can change your life. Let me give you an example.

I have a patient on my hospice team who is 75 years old. He was a successful businessman who worked hard to make money so that he could enjoy retirement. He even worked on Christmas Eve. His daughter told me that when she was young, she had to wait for daddy to come home in the early hours of Christmas day to open presents. Now this man has cancer and is on hospice care.

His wife is very sad and upset. This is her thinking: "He worked so hard all his life; now we have enough savings; this is the time to travel and enjoy life; but look what happened; it is not fair; why is God punishing me like this?" She is angry, anxious and depressed.

The daughter, on the other hand, thinks differently: She said: "I feel sad that my parents cannot enjoy their retirement together; but I am not angry with God; we should not postpone life today, to enjoy it later; the 'later' might never come; each day has to be lived to its fullest." The daughter is much more at peace. She has a positive outlook on the situation based on her spiritual thinking.

Two different ways of thinking about the same situation. If the wife could "change her mind" about the reality, she could experience some peace. That is what repentance really means. Change your mind so that you can change your life. Apostle Paul says in Romans: "Do not conform any longer to the patterns of this world, but be transformed by the renewal of your mind."(12:2)

Don't be afraid to use your mind in spiritual life. Faith is important, but we are supposed to have a faith that seeks understanding. Unfortunately, for many people, mind or the brain is the least used organ in their body. When it comes to spiritual life, many people refuse to engage the mind. They don't think about what they believe or why they believe what they believe; they just believe either because it is the tradition or they are told by preachers what to believe. An open mind is capable of deep reflection and it has the capacity to engage in new and creative ways of thinking and understanding. Let me tell you a story.

A man who was on a scavenger hunt knocks at the door of Mr. Smith at midnight. The man says to Mr. Smith: "I am on a scavenger hunt; I need a piece of wood 3 feet by 7 feet and I will pay you $10,000 for it." Mr. Smith thinks for a moment: "It is midnight; *Home Depot* and *Lowes* are closed. There is no wood in the garage." He tells the man: "I am sorry, I can't help you, there is no wood in the house."

The man leaves and Mr. Smith goes back to bed; but he can't sleep. He had all kinds of thoughts going through his mind; "If only I had bought some wood during my last trip to the *Home Depot,* I would have been rich by $10,000 now." He thought about all the things he could have done with that money. His fantasy went on and on and he began to fall asleep. Suddenly, Mr. Smith jumped out of his bed, saying to himself...*the door... the door...* he had half a dozen doors in his house, all of them made of wood, measuring, and 3 by 7. He could have removed a door from its hinges and given to the man!

What happened here is, that in Mr. Smith's mind, when he heard the word "wood," he could only think of wood on the shelves of *Home Depot* or *Lowes*. His mind did not have the capacity to expand and include the fact that the door is in fact, wood. He had put door only in the category of door and wood only something he finds in *Home Depot*; his mind could not think "outside the box."

We do this all the time in our spiritual life and that is why our faith gets stunted, our spirituality becomes choreographed to fit the confines of the church, our experience of God is limited to the reading of one holy book and our encounter with Jesus is often within the four walls of the church. As a result, we rarely feel the joy and freedom of the children of God. Spirituality becomes a boring and monotonous enterprise. The season of Lent comes and goes, but nothing really changes. It doesn't have to be that way.

Let me tell you the story of a lady I met the other day. Let us call her Susan. She was a 60 year old widow; she attended daily Mass and received communion. She never dated for years, until she met this nice guy and they fell in love and he wanted to marry her. But there was a problem. He is a divorcee. The Catholic Church does not approve of divorce and if you marry a divorcee, you cannot receive communion.

So Susan was in a dilemma. She could not imagine not being able to receive communion for the rest of her life; but she also wanted to marry this man. So she went to see her parish priest. Unfortunately, the priest was so legalistic and could not think outside the rules of Church. He told her that if she married this man, she should not receive communion. Susan was devastated.

So this nice lady wanted a second opinion. She approached a priest who was a friend. That priest told her: "I can't marry you in the church; go and get married elsewhere and let me see what I can do." So, she found a protestant minister, who blessed her marriage in the club house of her condo.

The next day, the couple came to the church, the priest took them inside and gave them a blessing and gave her permission to receive communion, but told her, "Don't tell anyone that I did this for you."

The woman was very confused. She told me that every time she approached the communion table, she was afraid and uncomfortable, worrying and wondering if Jesus would approve of her and come into her heart.

What is going on here? The first priest, in his mind, could not reconcile the reality of divorce and communion at the same time; the second priest did so, but was not comfortable about it. They were thinking in either/or categories. They could not think of both. Their minds were mired in the teachings of the Church rather than the teachings of Jesus, which can be contradictory at times, but you need an open mind even to discuss that.

Let us see what would Jesus do in such a situation? Let's check the gospels: In Mark 10: 11, Jesus clearly says that divorce is bad.

"Whoever divorces his wife and marries another, commits adultery against her" and according to the Old Testament, adultery is a sin that deserves to be punished by stoning to death. Based on that passage, the priest concluded that this woman has sinned and she should not receive communion.

Now read the story of the Samaritan woman in John chapter 4. What is Jesus doing there? Against the consternation of his disciples and the utter surprise of the woman herself, Jesus enters into a dialogue with her. A man talking with a woman in public is bad enough; but here is a Jew talking to a Gentile, which is scandalous. And she is a divorcee too, which makes it beyond the pale of a holy man. She is not just divorced once, but five times, and the man she is now living with is not even her husband.

So, Jesus who teaches against divorce can at the same time enters into a dialogue with a woman who is divorced five times. Jesus could do this because he had a mind that was open to the mercies of God, to the mysteries of our existence, and to the possibility of change. This is the Jesus I want to get know; this is the Jesus I want to follow; this is the Jesus I want to worship, a Jesus who can entertain the opposites in life, a Jesus who can deal with contradictions in life, a Jesus with a wide open mind that can accommodate the complex realities of complicated lives.

Let me add a word about the lady in the story. Why would she even go the priest to get permission to receive Jesus? This is because, in her thinking, the priest "controls" who Jesus should go to. How absurd is that? If she were to "change her thinking" and believe that the Jesus who came to seek not the just but the sinners would come to her heart, she could have received communion.

William James, the famous American spiritual writer said this: "The greatest discovery of my generation is that man can change his life simply by changing the attitude of his mind."

I just finished reading the biography of Steve Jobs by Walter Issacson. It is a huge book with nearly 700 pages. Steve Jobs was a genius often compared to Thomas Edison and Henry Ford. He had a phrase he always used when talking to his employees at *Apple*: **Think different.** (Grammatically it should be *think differently*, because it is an adverb). But Jobs wanted it to be *Think Different* to be "different" I guess.

Instead of thinking of the cell phone as a devise just to make calls (that is the traditional thinking about the phone), he wanted to think different. As a result he made the phone into a devise to listen to music, take pictures, browse the internet, send and receive emails, use as a calendar, clock, appointment book, stop watch, timer, album, note book, and GPS, play games, cook your dinner, mow your lawn and more, (I just made up the last two)…the i*Phone*. Steve Jobs used his mind to *think different* and brought into this world some very exciting products to change our lives in the ways we connect, communicate and interact.

Our excitement and innovation does not have to be confined to the material realm. Our spiritual life can be exciting too, if we are willing to repent. If we are willing to think different about our pre-conceived ideas about God, Jesus, the bible and life itself.

Very often, our minds are narrow, judgmental, opinionated, suspicious, revengeful, stubborn, small and even closed. As a result, we feel like victims, we see the world as a hostile place, and experience life as a struggle. It doesn't have to be that way.

Change your thinking and change your life; In gospel terms**, repent**. "Put on the mind of Christ and be transformed."

10. Why Good News People Live Bad News Lives
Text: Luke 4: 16-21

He went up to Nazareth, where he had been brought up, and on the Sabbath day he went into the synagogue, as was his custom. And he stood up to read. The scroll of the prophet Isaiah was handed to him. Unrolling it, he found the place where it is written: "The Spirit of the Lord is on me, because he has anointed me to preach good news to the poor. He has sent me to proclaim freedom for the prisoners and recovery of sight for the blind, to release the oppressed, to proclaim the year of the Lord's favor."

Then he rolled up the scroll, gave it back to the attendant and sat down. The eyes of everyone in the synagogue were fastened on him, and he began by saying to them, "Today this scripture is fulfilled in your hearing."

Christians believe that they are the people of the *Good News*. The foundation of Christianity is the good news. Jesus told the disciples to go and preach the good news. The whole purpose of the missionary journeys of Paul to Rome and Corinth and Galatia and other places were to preach the good news.

Through the centuries, Christian missionaries have traveled the lands, because they believed they had the good news and they wanted to share it with those who didn't. Last month, one of the elders from my church traveled to Thailand to preach and pray with missionaries there.

So we are sure we have the good news. Some people are even proud that they have it. The other day I was talking with a woman who attends the Christian Life Center in our city. She told me in no uncertain terms that those who don't believe in Jesus as their personal savior are going to hell for eternity. She had no doubt about that, because she had the good news and people belonging to other religions did not.

Many people describe America as a *Christian Nation* because it is based on the Judeo-Christian principles which include of course the good news of Jesus. Half of the world, which is about 3 billion Christians, believes that they have the good news.

So my question is, why is our country and the world in such a bad shape? Why do many Christians live unhappy and unfulfilled lives, barely making it in this valley of tears, hoping that after death, it will all be different because they will go to heaven to be with God forever?

Why do people live bad news lives? We can live bad news lives in two ways: First, by being bad towards us, and secondly, by being bad towards others. If you are living your life as if you have received some bad news--angry, upset, short tempered, moody, and not so pleasant to be around, you are living a bad news life. If you get up every morning with no energy and enthusiasm, and look at the world with negative lens, you are living a bad news life. If you are anxious and stressed out about everything, feel no joy and experience a lot of uncertainty and fear, you are living a bad news life. The good news of Jesus has not penetrated your life.

Secondly, we can be "bad news" to other people. When we are bad news to ourselves it is so hard to be good news to others. Bin Laden was bad news to the whole western world. Hitler was bad news to 6 million Jews. These are two examples on a grand scale. But each of us is capable of being bad news to the people around us, the people we live with work with and interact with.

We know that despite the fact that the earth is populated by 3 billion people who claim to have the good news, the world is not a paradise.

According to UNICEF, 22,000 children die each day due to poverty. And they "die quietly in some of the poorest villages on earth, far removed from the scrutiny and the conscience of the world." Being meek and weak in life makes these dying multitudes even more invisible in death. Nearly a billion people entered the 21st century unable to read a book or sign their names. Less than one per cent of what the world spent every year on weapons was needed to put every child into school by the year 2000 and yet it didn't happen.

Infectious diseases continue to blight the lives of the poor across the world. An estimated 40 million people are living with HIV/AIDS, with 3 million deaths in 2009. Every year there are 350–500 million cases of malaria, with 1 million fatalities: Africa accounts for 90 percent of malarial deaths.

At present, 3 billion people live on less than $2 per day while 1.3 billion get by on less than $1 per day.

So that is the status about poverty. What about wars in this world? If you count all current conflicts where hostilities are still present and conflicts that have ceased hostilities but are still unresolved, there are approximately 31. This includes the obvious conflicts in Afghanistan as well as conflicts like the Korean War that have cease fires in place but are still unresolved and the two sides are still staring at the barrel of guns.

As I said, 3 billion occupants of this world are supposedly "good news people" and of course that includes us. So, why is the world such a largely bad news place? Why there is such abject poverty, war, hatred, killings, divisions, disunity, homophobia, and partisanship? Why would those who claim to be followers of the "Prince of Peace" amass guns and assault weapons whose only purpose is to hurt and kill? What are they afraid of if they claim to understand the message of the risen Jesus: "Fear not."

My theory is that we don't even know what the good news really is, let alone understand what it really means!

What is the good news of Jesus? When I asked this question in a bible study group, a lady said: "Jesus died for our sins thereby giving us eternal life in heaven after we die; our salvation is guaranteed in Jesus."

Let me clarify something; Jesus did not **die** on the cross; he was **killed** on the cross. What is the difference, you might ask. There is a big difference. It is not like Jesus woke up the morning of that Friday, and decided that he was going to die on the cross and asked the soldiers to pin him down and pierce his hands, legs and heart so that he could just die, something like an assisted suicide?

Jesus was brutally murdered by the authorities because his message and ideas were a threat to their very survival. The Pharisees did not want to give up their idea of religion. The Romans did not want to give up their seat of power. Jesus was a threat to both. They wanted to get rid of the troublemaker, so they executed him. In that sense, Jesus didn't die so much for the sins of the world as he died because of the sins of the world. In other words, Jesus was killed **because of our sins**, rather than **for our sins**.

It makes us responsible for his execution rather than beneficiaries of his death.

This understanding will hopefully help us not to kill Jesus today through our hate, prejudice and insensitivity towards other people who are Jesus in disguise, because, "whatever you did to the least of my brothers, you did it to me." By the way, being good to the people around you is a way to live the good news.

So, back to the topic of good news. What is the good news of Jesus? To find that, you have to search the gospels. In the first three gospels, Jesus appears on the scene when he was about 30 years old. He is baptized in the river Jordan; he is tempted for three days in the desert and after that he officially begins his public ministry.

What are the first words that come out of his mouth? According to Mt: 4:17, they are, *Repent, for the Kingdom of Heaven is near.* In Mk: 1:14, Jesus says: *The Kingdom of God is near; repent and believe the good news.* The fact that the kingdom of God is ***near*** is the good news. Mathew and Mark do not explain what the kingdom is. In Luke we get an explanation. Jesus does not use the word kingdom in his inaugural address as recorded in Luke 4. Like in Mark and Mathew, Jesus begins to preach after the baptism and temptation. He goes to a synagogue and reads from the book of Isaiah.

The Spirit of the Lord is upon me because he has anointed me to preach the good news to the poor.

So what is this good news? The next lines unpack it: The good news is that Jesus is sent to "proclaim freedom for the prisoners;" the good news is that Jesus is sent to bring "recovery of sight for the blind;" the good news is that Jesus has come "to release the oppressed." The good news is that Jesus has come "to proclaim the year of the Lord's favor."

So the good news is that if you are a prisoner to your addictions and narrow mindedness and prejudices and hatreds, your one track mind, your arrogant nationalism, your thinking that everybody who disagrees with you should be destroyed, Jesus has come to help you change that.

The good news is that if you are blind to the beauty of God's creation around you, if you are blind to the goodness of people in the world, if you are blind to the blessings you already have, if you are blind to the poverty around you, if you are blind to the needs of others, then Jesus has come to heal your blindness and open your eyes.

The good news is that the Kingdom is near. This is not a far away Kingdom, a location beyond the clouds, but a reality right here in the midst of our world. A Kingdom of love, peace, joy, patience, goodness, kindness and a sense of well being.

The good news is that Jesus has come to proclaim the year of the Lord's favor when debts are forgiven, mercy is shown to strangers, compassion is manifested, and peace and harmony prevail among the people.

The good news is the person of Jesus. Remember when he was born, the angel announced to the shepherds: *I bring you good news of great joy to the people.* (Lk 2:10)

So to experience the good news, we have to get to **know the historical Jesus** and **follow** him.

Majority of Christians only know the **Christ of faith**, not the **historical Jesus**. They know him as the Son of God, begotten by the father, born of a virgin, and the second person of the Holy Trinity. According to David Galston, who by the way, has written a good book on this topic called, *Embracing the Human Jesus*, it is an "impressive resume." But, focusing on the divinity of Jesus has very little impact on our humanity. We will worship him in church and leave, but how can we follow the "second person of the Holy Trinity"?

We have to discover the **human Jesus** in the pages of the gospels who still has the power to transform our lives as he did the lives of Nicodemus, Zacheus, Jairus, Nathaniel, Mathew and a lot of others. Everyone who encountered Jesus was changed. We need to encounter Jesus and follow him rather than put him on a pedestal and worship him. Pedastalization of Jesus is the pathology of Christianity. We cannot be like Jesus unless we find out what Jesus was like. We have to change our whole mind-set about what it means to be a Christian. That is why the first word out of the mouth of Jesus was: **Repent.** But repent does not mean, feel sorry for your sins. It has nothing to do with feeling bad or sorry for anything.

The Greek word for repent is *metanoeo* which means, a *different mind*. You have to have a different mind about things. You have to change your thinking about things and align your mind with that of Jesus: **a new way of thinking and seeing the world**. As apostle Paul would say: "You have to put on the mind of Christ."

You have to think like Jesus, feel like Jesus and behave like Jesus. When you do that, you will start feeling the good news and that will lead you to being good news for others.

11. Are You a CINO?
Text: Galatians 5: 4-6, 13-15

You who are trying to be justified by law have been alienated from Christ; you have fallen away from grace. But by faith we eagerly await through the Spirit the righteousness for which we hope. For in Christ, Jesus neither circumcision nor uncircumcision has any value. The only thing that counts is faith expressing itself through love...You, my brothers, were called to be free. But do not use your freedom to indulge the sinful nature; rather, serve one another in love. The entire law is summed up in a single command: "Love your neighbor as yourself."

A man was being tailgated by a stressed out woman on a busy street. Suddenly the light turned yellow, just in front of him. He did the right thing by stopping at the crosswalk, even though he could have beaten the red light by accelerating through the intersection.

The tailgating woman was furious and honked her horn, screaming in frustration as she missed her chance to get through the intersection, dropping her cell phone and make up.

While she was still ranting and raving, she hears a tap on the window and looked up to see the face of a very serious police officer. The officer asked her to exit the car with her hands up. He took her to the police station where she was searched, finger printed, photographed and placed in a holding cell.

After a couple of hours, a policeman approached the cell and opened the door. She was escorted back to the booking desk where the arresting officer was sitting with her personal effects.

He said: "I am very sorry for this mistake; you see, I pulled up behind your car while you were blowing your horn, flipping off the guy in front of you, and cussing at him. Then I noticed the *WWJD* bumper sticker, the *Choose Life* license plate, the *Follow me to the Sunday School* bumper sticker and the custom plated Christian fish emblem on the trunk; naturally, I assumed, you had stolen the car."

Now this woman is a good example of a CINO. Christian In Name Only. She had all the external trappings of Christianity, but she did not act like a Christian.

Here is a news item from a Kansas City news paper, dated June 1, 2009: *51 year old Scott Roeder, a Christian Terrorist, entered the Reformation Lutheran Church Sunday morning and shot congregation usher and abortion doctor George Tiller once through the head. He pointed his gun at others in making his escape. Not only a Christian, Roeder was also a "Freemason", an offshoot of the libertarian movement who believe they are not subject to any state or federal laws.*

Scott Roeder is another example of a good CINO.

Let me give you one more story. Few weeks ago, CNN had a feature called *Extremists or Patriots*. It was the story of a militia in Michigan. Members of the Militia don't talk to media but this particular family did. The family consisted of a husband and wife and their six children, between the ages of five and seventeen. And they had 22 guns in their home. I am not making this up. On Saturday, the man takes his two oldest children, a 17 year old girl and a 15 year old boy, for target practice. And on Sundays, the family goes to church.

They said they celebrated Christmas and Easter, said their prayers and read their bible. As a matter of fact, the Bible was placed next to the gun that was locked up in a shelf in the family room. Call me crazy, but I have no idea what a gun and a bible has to do with each other. Or what guns and Christianity have to do with each other? Or what does churches and guns have in common? There is a pastor in Kentucky, Ken Pagano of New Bethel Church, who asked the members of his congregation to bring guns for a celebration.

"As a Christian pastor I believe that without a deep-seeded belief in God and firearms, this country would not be here," Pagano told ABC News. "I'm not ashamed of that fact. I'm proud of it."

The celebration scheduled for Sunday, June 27, will feature *You Tube* Videos promoting gun safety and will ask congregants to join in singing patriotic songs, according to Pagano.

"This will basically be a display," said Pagano, who owns two hand guns, a Walther P99 and a Sig Sauer 229.

"There will be extra security present during the celebration," said Pagano, "and guns will be checked to make sure they are unloaded prior to entering the church."

While Pagano says that the majority of the congregation voted in favor of the celebration, others are not as happy.

Paul Helmke, the president of the Brady Campaign to Prevent Gun Violence, said that "encouraging people to bring guns to a church is a contradiction in terms." You think?

"Christ tells us to put down the sword and this pastor seems to be encouraging them to take up the sword," said Helmke.

Pastor Pagano, in my opinion, is another good example of a CINO. He can call himself a Christian pastor, but I don't think he has anything to do with Christ. I am sorry, I feel so passionately about this. There is no way you can justify the Jesus of the gospels and use of guns. What has it to do with Jesus who said,

"Love your enemies, and turn your other cheek if someone strikes you on your right cheek?"

Someone might say, but "I have the Second Amendment rights to own a firearm." But the question is what is more important: The *Second Amendment* or the *Ten Commandments*? What is more important for a Christian: The Bill of Rights for the Sermon on the Mount? How do you reconcile the *Second Amendment* with the *Fifth Commandment?*

Gun is a symbol of fear and insecurity. As a follower of Jesus who advised us not to be afraid, I will never own or use a gun. I have nothing that needs to be protected at gun point and there is no cause out there that I am willing to kill for, and that includes my safety and that of my family.

Many people value their faith for the comfort and the lift they receive from it. But when all is said and done, Jesus is largely forgotten or sidelined. His teachings and the example of his life plays only a marginal role in the lives of great many Christians. They may love the sound of his name, but their priorities, goals, loyalties and vision of life come from some source other than Jesus.

I like to quote my pastor, Craig Watts, who feels passionately about this:

It is a tragedy that Christians celebrate Jesus as the way of their salvation but they don't embrace him as their way of life. They see Jesus as someone who washes them from their sins with his blood, and grants them salvation after death. They rarely see Jesus as someone for whom it is worth shedding the blood, leaving aside concerns about one's own safety, security and prosperity.

They look at the cross to save them, but they don't allow the cross to shape them. It is easy to look at a cross and pray, "Jesus, you are my Lord and Savior," but it is hard to follow the WAY of the cross. Jesus calls his followers to live cruciform lives. He said: "If anyone wants to come after me, he must deny himself, take up his cross and follow me." There is no mincing of words here. First Peter, 2:21 repeats that call: "It is for this you were called, since Christ suffered for you and left you an example, to have you follow in his footsteps."

It is in taking up the cross and following in his footsteps that we find our deepest joy and our truest fulfillment. But many Christians forget this completely. Many Christians wear the cross merely as an ornament. One latest example that comes to mind is that of Carie Prejan. Do you know who she is?

She is *Miss California*, a participant in the *Miss America Pageant*. Her crown was taken away from her and she was kicked out of the beauty pageant organization, because of a huge controversy about gay marriage. She said that as a Christian she could not approve of gay marriage. She wears a cross around her neck. Fair enough; I can appreciate that, but she did at least two things which I think are very un-Christian.

She accepted $5000 for a breast augmentation from the California Beauty Pageant. Now, is breast augmentation a Christian value? I am not sure, but we can debate that. But she did something else that is definitely un-Christian. She made about 20 sex tapes of herself, and sent them to her boyfriend with whom she had broken up, to win him back. She says she is a Christian, she wears a cross. I wonder!

The word Christian means Christ-like. How would things be if Christians were really *Christians*? First of all, we would keep Jesus front and center. We would continuously open the gospels and consider what Jesus taught and did. We would ponder his life and actions. We would allow his story to penetrate out lives.

Have you noticed that most of the Christian preachers on television and radio usually read and quote from the Old Testament? If it is the New Testament, it is mostly from letters of Paul or the book of *Revelations*. They use the book of *Leviticus* to chastise the gays; they use letters of Paul to tell us about an angry God who needs to be expiated by the blood of his son so that our sins can be washed away. They talk about the end of the world in the book of *Revelations* to scare people. If you scare people you can control them and extract money from them.

But they rarely read or quote from the four *gospels*. That is where you find the living Jesus who makes some serious demands on us. It is very difficult to follow that Jesus, but it is easy to worship the almighty God of the Old Testament.

Let me use again the powerful words of my pastor, Craig Watts, to conclude this sermon:

*If Christians were really Christian, we would speak more truthfully, forgive more radically, give more generously, love more boundlessly and live more non-violently. Quite simply, if Christians were more **Christian**, we would be a lot more like Jesus and a lot less like everyone else. In other words, we would be the "salt of the earth and the light of the world" Jesus said his followers should be.*

*If Christians were really **Christian**, the Church would be the bright and shining city on a hill that no nation ever has been or ever will be. God wants to use us in wonderful ways. We have a high and holy calling. If we keep our eyes on Jesus, there is no end to how God can use us, bless us and bless others through us. Let us always support and encourage each other to be people who are fully and really **Christian.***

12. Christian or Disciple?
Text: Luke 14:25-27, 34-35

Large crowds were traveling with Jesus, and turning to them he said: "If anyone comes to me and does not hate his father and mother, his wife and children, his brothers and sisters—yes, even his own life—he cannot be my disciple. And anyone who does not carry his cross and follow me cannot be my disciple...Salt is good, but if it loses its saltiness, how can it be made salty again? It is fit neither for the soil nor for the manure pile; it is thrown out. "He who has ears to hear, let him hear."

As you know I was a Catholic priest for 13 years prior to leaving and getting married. In the beginning of our marriage, my wife and I attended Mass in a Catholic parish. But after a while, it became increasingly hard to just sit in the pew and go through the motions. So we decided to try out the Protestant churches, but which one? Growing up in India, where Catholics are the majority among Christians, I had hardly any contact with Protestants.

I knew the names of Protestant groups here: The Lutherans, the Methodists, the Presbyterians, the Baptists, but I had never worshiped in any of their churches. There are 18 churches in a four mile radius of our house. So we went church shopping every Sunday and visited about ten different churches. After the service, we would go out for brunch and talk about our worship experience. We would evaluate the sermon, the congregation, how friendly and open they are, etc. The fact of the matter is that I was not thrilled with any of the major churches.

They seemed too narrow to me. They seemed to follow the ideology of their founder more than that of Jesus himself. For example, the Lutheran church came into being due to Martin Luther and the Lutherans usually follow the teachings of Luther. I know it is not true, but the name kind of suggests that.

The same with the Methodists; John Calvin is the founder of Methodists and his teachings are prominent in the Methodist churches. Again, they seem to follow Calvin more than Jesus; I know it is not true, but the name kind of suggests that.

Take Presbyterianism. It was founded by John Knox in Scotland in 1557, and the standard expression of doctrines and faith can be found in the Westminster Confession of Faith. There is nothing wrong with that *per se*. If you want to study the Westminster Confession of Faith formulated by a group of clergy, that is fine. But I want to be part of a church whose standard of faith and doctrines are found in the gospels, not in a "Westminster Confession of Faith" or any such document.

There are three billion Christians in the world and they belong to about 36,000 different denominations. Among Baptists alone, there are 94 sub-groups. Catholics for example, come in 242 different flavors. Most of you are familiar with the Roman Catholics which is the largest group. But there are 241 independent Catholic churches that are not under the jurisdiction of the Pope.

So, we continued our church shopping and finally walked into Royal Palm Christian Church in Coral Springs, Florida. We were immediately impressed by the warmth and friendliness of the congregation. But more importantly, I was very happy with the name of the denomination. It was not named after any human person, like a Luther or a Calvin or a John Knox or a John Wesley. It is named after Jesus Himself. The denomination is called *Disciples of Christ*.

I don't think there is a better name for a church than Disciples of Christ, because that is what we are called to be. It is our reason for being.

When I study the history of Christianity and observe its current status, one thing is very clear: the world is full of Christians but very few disciples. There are three billion Christians in this world, but only a tiny minority of them are disciples.

What is the difference? What is the difference between a Disciple and a Christian? The difference is huge. I like to take a few Sundays to explain the deeper meaning and implications of discipleship and I like to use some ideas from a book, *Mere Discipleship, by* Lee Camp to do that.

But today's sermon is mainly to explain the difference between a Disciple and a Christian. And I like to use a story from *Mere Discipleship* to show this difference rather than didactic teaching which is often boring.

It is a story of the genocide in Rwanda. Rwanda is a small country in Africa with a population of about ten million people. The two major tribes in that country are the Tutsis and the Hutus. In 1994, ethnic tensions between these two tribes erupted into widespread slaughter, with neighbor killing neighbor.

The national army, vigilante groups and average citizens hunted those of different ethnic identity. Their enemies were hacked to death using machetes. Thus Rwanda became the site of genocide unlike any in recent history. As many as 800,000 men, women and children were slaughtered within a period of three months.

There is one piece of information I haven't told you about Rwanda. And that is: Rwanda is the most Christian country in Africa. 94 percent of its population claims church affiliation. 56.7 percent are Catholics and 37.1 percent are Protestants. It is not like the Tutsis were Muslims killing the Hutus who were Christians; or vice verse. Both tribes are Christians.

Rwanda was often cited as a case study for the Success of Christian Missions. In the 1930s, Western missionaries preached Christianity there, and converted the tribes and made them Christians.

But the genocide demonstrated in a horrific and graphic way that the western Christianity imported in to the heart of Africa apparently failed to create communities of DISCIPLES. When push came to shove, the Jesus who taught his disciples to "love your neighbor" was missing when young men were hacking old men, women and children to death, simply because these neighbors belong to a different tribe.

A church is usually considered a safe place. We know of churches acting as "safe havens" for immigrants and refugees. But in Rwanda, Catholic priests belonging to the Tutsi tribe invited the Hutus into their churches under the guise of giving them sanctuary. Once they were in, the priests would alert their tribesmen who would massacre those people inside the churches.

The fact of the matter is that the "gospel" imported into Rwanda failed to challenge the ethnic identities of its "converts." They became Christians, but many remained first and foremost a Hutu or a Tutsi. Had they become disciples, the genocide would not have happened, because a true disciple of Jesus cannot kill another human being.

Jesus did not use the word Christian to describe his followers. There were no Christians during the time of Jesus. Jesus was not a Christian. In fact, you don't find the word Christian in the gospels. The first time followers of Jesus were called Christians was in Antioch, and we find that in the 11th chapter of the *Acts of the Apostles*.

Today, the word Christian means member of the religion called Christianity which is one of the three major religions of

the world. For many, it is more of an organizational membership than a way of life.

For the first three centuries of the Church, the Roman Empire ignored or killed Christians. Christians were a persecuted minority. But that changed when Emperor Constantine became a Christian. The persecution stopped. Christianity was made the only legal religion in the Empire. From that arose Christendom, an alliance between the Church and the Empire. The Christian Church gained glory and status.

At the outset it may look like a good thing. What is wrong with some power, and glory and status in the world, you might ask? The problem is that every time the Church enters into alliance with the state, the church always loses its soul. You cannot be friends with the State and still criticize it.
I remember the dinner President Bush had with the Catholic Bishops in Washington in 2003. It is an annual ritual. They shake hands and take photos and schmooze. On March 23rd that year, the war on Iraq was declared. Not one US Catholic bishop spoke against it. When you compromise with the state you lose the ability to be the conscience of the state. Jesus was able to criticize and challenge the political authorities of his time, because he stood away from them with clarity of vision and purity of character. We cannot say that for many of the so called followers of Jesus today.

So, that is what happened in the third century when Christianity was elevated to the status of state religion. Christianity lost is biblical emphasis on discipleship and replaced it with an emphasis on religious ritual. "Church" instead of meaning the disciples living as a "body of Christ" became more of an organization.

For many people, being a Christian is a badge of honor. It is membership in a respectable club. I have heard Christians say, I am so glad I am not a Muslim.

The irony is that a country can be dubbed Christian, and yet it could be very un-Christ like. Or a person can claim to be a Christian but engage in some very un-Christ like behavior. That is why Dietrich Bonheoffer once said: ***Christianity without discipleship is Christianity without Christ.***

Attending church every Sunday does not make someone a disciple, like standing in a garage does not make you a car. It is a good start, but it is not the end.

So I have a question for you today. Are you a Worshiper, Admirer, Believer or Follower of Jesus? They mean very different things. When it comes to your relationship to Jesus, Are you a worshiper, admirer, believer or follower?
Someone can be a worshiper and not a follower. For example Hitler and Mussolini were worshipers of Jesus. They were Christians, but not disciples.

You can be an admirer and not a follower. Hugo Chavez and Fidel Castro are admirers of Jesus, but they are not disciples.

You can be a believer and not a follower. There are millions of them. Serial killer Ted Bundy and Oklahoma City bomber Timothy McVeigh were believers; they were Christians, but not disciples.

In the aftermath of 9/11, the late Jerry Farwell said: "We should blow up all the Muslims in the world in the name of Jesus our Lord."

We should always aspire to be a follower or a disciple.

I know why we would rather be Christians and not Disciples, because discipleship is hard. A disciple has to deny himself, take up his cross and follow Jesus.

A disciple has to think like Jesus, behave like Jesus, love like Jesus, forgive like Jesus, suffer like Jesus.

Discipleship is something that happens to us when Jesus really invades our lives.

Christianity is something that happens around us when Jesus stands outside of us, like an ornament on a Christmas tree.

When Jesus invades our lives the whole landscape of our lives will change. Being a Christian is a very superficial thing. Discipleship is harder and deeper.

Let us pray that our Christianity grow into discipleship each day.

13. Adam and Eve: The Untold Story
Text: Genesis 1: 26-27

Then God said, "Let us make man in our image, in our likeness, and let them rule over the fish of the sea and the birds of the air, over the livestock, over all the earth, and over all the creatures that move along the ground." So God created man in his own image, in the image of God he created him; male and female he created them.

When you hear the names *Adam* and *Eve* what is the story that comes to your mind? The most predominant story line is that Adam was created from the clay of the earth. Then God decided that he should have a companion, because it is not good for a man to be alone. So, God puts Adam to sleep (the first case of anesthesia in the Bible) and did surgery on his side: took out a rib and created the woman and Adam named her, Eve. They were placed in the Garden of Eden. There was a tree in the middle of the garden, the "tree of knowledge of good and evil." They were told not to eat the fruit of that tree which apparently was an apple (the bible doesn't say that).

One day, the serpent comes along and tempts Eve and she eats the fruit; she gives one to Adam and he too eats it; when God finds that out, He becomes very angry. He comes to the garden; Adam and Eve are hiding behind the bushes because they were afraid and naked. God was upset they disobeyed his command. He gets mad; first he punishes the serpent by cursing him to crawl on his belly for the rest of his life; it sounds like the serpent used to walk on his legs and eat steak before that; (but that is another discussion). Then he punishes the woman with painful child birth and punishes Adam with hard work on earth. And of course, they are thrown out of the paradise.

Then God feels guilty about over reacting, maybe? He felt guilty for about a thousand years; that is a long time for a God to get over his anger and guilt. So centuries later, God sends his only son, Jesus to save humanity from their sins caused by the sin of Adam and Eve, which is called the original sin. Jesus comes and dies on the cross and saves us through his blood.

This is the story line that we have been told for centuries. This story continues to be told from many pulpits. You hear this story from TV and radio preachers. If you listen to *Moody Radio*, this is the main story you hear all the time. Pat Robertson talks about it on his TV program called *The 700 Club*.

There is nothing wrong with the story itself. It is in the bible. But this story has not served the world well. Look around you. What do you see? Is our life any better because of this story? There are so many wars, so much poverty, so much greed, and plenty of disharmony and disunity in the world. The world is not a better place because of this story.

Maybe we need to tell a different story about who we are and how we came into this world and what we are supposed to do with our lives. Now you may be saying silently, "Oh no, Paul, don't make up a story." We know you are a progressive thinker, but don't tell us a story that you made up to confuse us; besides, we are Christians, and we believe in the bible. We can only believe a story if it is in the bible."

I respect that; as a matter of fact, I don't want to tell a story that is not in the bible either. The story that I am going to tell you is in the bible, but it is rarely told. I listen to a lot of religious radio and TV, but I hear no one telling this story. So let me tell you, I did not make it up. It is not taken from any modern book or magazine.
It is in the bible. Let us open our bibles.

Many people don't know that there are TWO creation stories in the bible. It is the second story that gets all the attention. As I said, our whole history of salvation is built up around the second story. The main thrust of that story, is the fall of Adam and Eve. The creation of the world is described in few verses. But the creation of Adam and Eve are very detailed. You can read it in Genesis 2:4 through the entire chapter three.

Now, let us read the first story, which is rarely told: From the start of Genesis chapter 1 till chapter 2:3. In this story, the first 25 verses are details about each day of creation of the universe: Creation of night and day, sun and moon and stars, waters and rivers, vegetation, trees and plants, living creatures, animals etc. and finally, in two verses, 26 & 27, is the story of the creation of humans.

Then God said: "Let us make man in our image; in our likeness, and let them rule over the fish of the sea and the birds of the air, over the livestock, over all the earth, and over all the creatures that move along the ground: SO GOD CREATED MAN IN HIS OWN IMAGE, IN THE IMAGE OF GOD HE CREATED HIM, MALE AND FEMALE HE CREATED THEM.

That is it; so simple yet so powerful.

There is no mention of making clay; there is no mention of removing a rib from the side of Adam. There is no insinuation of secondary status for the woman. In the second story, the woman is created AFTER the man was created, like an afterthought, like a helper to man; someone who can help with the loneliness of man. She is not the main character; she is in a supporting role.

Is it possible that throughout history, women were treated as second class citizens because we focused on this second story of creation of humans? Is it possible that women were considered the weaker sex and as objects of sexual exploitation by men, because we focused on this story? Is it possible that women had voting rights in this country only since 1920 because we focused on this story? Is it possible that in Saudi Arabia, women are not allowed to drive a car because of this story? Is it possible that in Afghanistan, women need a male companion when she goes out in public and she has to cover her face with a burkha? Maybe this story has something to do with the fact that America never had a woman president? Think about it.

In the first creation story there is no indication of creation of woman as an afterthought; not as a helper, not as an accessory to man, not in a supporting role, but as an equal partner with the same calling and dignity as man himself.

You have heard the phrase "I am who Am." When Moses encountered God in the burning bush, he asked for his name and God said: I AM WHO AM. When God called Moses, he answered, "Here I am." When God called prophet Isaiah, he answered "Here I am."

Moses and Isaiah were to act in the world as agents of God; they were to lead the people of God on behalf of God; they were to be partners WITH God; they were called to be co-creators of a new Kingdom in this world.

They responded to that call by declaring HERE I AM. When they used that phrase, they were attaching themselves to the great I AM who is God. They were empowered to do that because they believed that they were partners and co-creators with God.

But look at how Adam responded to God when his name was called in the garden after he ate the fruit. He could not respond, "HERE I AM," because he felt ashamed, afraid, and embarrassed. He thought he was unworthy because he was made of clay, a weak and helpless sinner. He felt estranged and separate from God; he did not feel part of God to say HERE I AM. Every time we use the phrase, "I AM" to introduce ourselves, we are actually introducing ourselves as agents of God, as manifestations of God, as representatives of God.

When we say, *I am* Paul, *I am* Dolores, *I am* Cheryl, *I am* Jim, *I am* Pat, *I am* Tyler, *I am* Rick, *I am* Bill, we are attaching the name of God to our name and declaring a divine connection. Your small "*I am*" is part of the Big I AM who is God. You are establishing a link with God.

What you are saying is: "I am coming into your life with the love and compassion of God; I am coming to you as the presence of God for you, right here, today, right now. Jesus has called me to be the light of the world to be a light for your today.

It is a huge responsibility. It is a privilege and honor that was given to us at creation when God created us in his image and likeness. I invite you to live your life from that vantage point, not from the vantage point of our so called *fallen* state.

I know it is so hard for you to comprehend that you are god. It is mainly due to two reasons. First you think you are a weak sinner, made of clay. That is because you are focusing on the second creation story of the Bible. But if you focus on the first creation story, you will find out that you are not a weak sinner but someone created in God's image.

God is the Creator with the capital **G** and capital **C**, but you are **god and co-creator**, with a small **g** and small **c**: a limited, localized, personalized version of God.

As Neale Donald Walsch would say:

You are not a mere speck of dust on the cosmic floor, unworthy to be even seen, much less celebrated; you are big and important, and yes, a glorious part of an ever ongoing

expression of Divinity.

So I invite you focus on the first creation story of man found in Genesis chapter one and claim your place in the universe as an Image of God, as an extension of the Big I AM. Life will change dramatically for you and for those around you.

14. Not Just Human
Text: 1 Corinthians 6: 19-20

Do you not know that your body is a temple of the Holy Spirit, who is in you, whom you have received from God? You are not your own; you were bought at a price. Therefore honor God with your body.

I want to tell you the story of an elderly man who went to the doctor for his annual physical. The doctor runs some tests and says: "Everything seems to be OK, physically; what about mentally? For example, how is your connection to God?"

Man: "Oh, me and God, we are very tight; we have a special bond, He is good to me; every night when I get up and go to the bathroom, he turns ON the light for me; and when I leave, he turns it OFF." The doctor was amazed.

He calls the man's wife: "You are a lucky woman; your husband is very spiritual; he has this special connection with God." "What do you mean?" asks the wife.

"He tells me that every night when he goes to the bathroom, God turns the light ON and OFF for him. Is that true?"

"It has nothing to do with God; he has been peeing in the refrigerator."

Old age is a funny stage of life, and that is why nobody wants to get old. We try our best to hide our age or lie about our age. There are many age hiding industries in the world. Let us start on the top. There is hair coloring, hair restoration, hair transplants and wigs. It is an 8 billion dollars a year business in the United States alone. I use to contribute to that industry, by purchasing *Just for Men*. Then there is plastic surgery, a 10 billion dollars a year industry.

If these artificial methods are non-verbal denials of age, there are verbal denials, too. I had a patient in an ALF who refused to reveal her age on her birthday. She was 74 years old, but she would say "today is the 25th anniversary of my 49th birthday."

With the low numbers of 25 and 49 she thought she could somehow camouflage the big number 74. It is an auditory illusion. Your aching joints and sagging body won't pay any attention to that. I had another patient who was 95. She was sharp as a tack but physically frail. We suggested that she use a wheelchair to go to the dining room. She refused. She was too proud to appear in public on a wheelchair which made her look old.

A few years ago, I used to deny my age, too. When my kids were young I used to take them to the pool. My son Tommy had this habit of telling people the ages of his parents. "My mommy is 35 years old and my daddy is 47 years old." Judy and I are 12 years apart. I did not want people to know that I was a cradle grabber. So I told Tommy that I was only 40. And I stayed 40 for a few years until he started school and began to figure out numbers. Then I told him the truth. I also stopped taking him to the pool.

In the past, when people asked how old I was, I used to say: "Too young for Medicare and too old for women to care." I was so mad when I got a letter from AARP inviting me to join. For me, AARP is synonymous with Social Security, Medicare, Century Village and early bird dinners.

I am sure you have many age related stories and experiences. Why are we so afraid of aging? Fear of death is part of it. I belong to this men's group that meets twice a month and all of us are in our 50's. One of the members said that he is not too happy to be in his 50s which means that more than half of his life is over and if he is lucky, there may be another good 20 years left, if that much.

So, some of the anxiety about aging is due to the fear that life is coming to its end. But much of age related anxiety is due to our physical appearance. We don't like what we see in the mirror.

And it is due to the false belief that we are this body. I say false because we are not our body. We have a body, but we are *not* our body.

This awareness hit me hard a few years ago, when I was watching TV. Oprah was doing a TV series with a spiritual teacher named Eckhart Tolle. The series was based on his book, *A New Earth, Awakening to Your Life's Purpose*, which by the way, is a great book. He has another good book called *The Power of Now*.

During the interview, Oprah asked Tolle how old he was. And his answer to that question was very profound. I had never heard anybody answer that question the way he did.

With a calm demeanor and a smile on his face, Mr. Tolle said: "My body is 60 years old." Oprah had this jaw dropping look on her face. And I said: "Wow, what a great answer."

The implications of that answer are huge. What he meant was that his body is 60 but his soul is eternal. Soul has no age, because the soul is part of God. So when talking about your age, don't say, "I am 60 years old, or I am 35;" that is the wrong answer. Because "I am" is part of the big I AM who is God. Remember God's name in the Old Testament? When Moses asked Yahweh his name what he said was, "I AM WHO AM."

When I say, "I am Paul or I am Alice or I am Sheila," we are acknowledging our connection to that great I am who is God. *I am* not 60 years old, my body is; *I am* eternal.

Today, we are having a "Health Rock" at our church. You will hear a lot about the importance of taking care of your body through proper diet and exercise; you will also hear a lot about our physical problems such as obesity, high blood pressure, stress etc. Take part in the fair and gather information about becoming a healthier person.

But I have a secret for you. Take care of your soul first, and most of the body problems you are dealing with will soon disappear. It is ironic that some people will go to the gym 5 times a week but will never spend 15 minutes a day meditating or an hour a week to attend church. And they wonder why they are so frustrated and depressed about life in spite of having a healthy body.

Our primary identity is that we are *spiritual beings*: "We are spiritual beings with human experiences rather than human beings with spiritual experiences." This identity is innate to us; it is part and parcel of our whole make up. That is why the bible says, "We are created in the image and likeness of God." But how soon we forget that!

Most of the time, we operate on the principle that we are just humans. We may feel spiritual when we are in church or when we read the bible or say some prayers. But many people act like mere humans most of the time. We even have this expression: "I am only human," or, "we are just human." I hate that expression.

It is an excuse we have come up with to justify our unwillingness to live up to our divine potential. Every time we refuse to follow Jesus, or fail to manifest the divinity within us, we blame it on our humanity.

Jesus said to his followers: "You are called to be perfect as your heavenly father is perfect." At the outset, it sounds like a tall order, a utopian dream, totally beyond our reach. If so, why would Jesus say that? I think it is possible to journey towards that perfection, provided we do two things.

First of all, we have to erase from our minds the notion that we are *just human*. The fact that we are human is only part of the story. We have to say we are human-beings; it is a compound word. Neither of those words should stand alone. **By attaching being with a small 'b' to our humanity, we are sharing in the life of the Supreme Being with a capital B.**

It is not an arrogant attitude, but the reclaiming of a birthright given to us when we entered this world: we are created in the image and likeness of God.

So the bigger story is that we are souls. **SOUL** stands for *Singular Output of Universal Life*. Yes, we are localized expressions of divinity. That is why Paul tells us that our body is the temple of the Holy Spirit. We are moving containers of divine energy. Jesus would call us the light of the world.

If you can keep that truth alive in your consciousness all the time, your life will change. You will not be angry, depressed, jealous, unhappy, frustrated or upset with anything, because souls don't do any of that; humans do.

When you rearrange your life and start operating from that part of your being which is soul, everything around you will change. When you start looking at the problems and struggles of your life from the perspective of the soul, they become easy to face; forgiveness becomes easier, peace becomes possible and joy becomes a part of life.

Believe me, all those things we describe as problems in our life and in the world have one common denominator, our body: the needs, desires, pleasures, and attachments of the body. Take any problem, personal, national or international, there is a body connection.

The soul has no problems or issues; the soul is about love, peace, joy, patience, kindness and goodness, faithfulness, generosity and self-control.

So, I invite you to replace the "false label" HUMAN from your life and let the original label SOUL manifest itself to the world. Your peace and joy will be directly proportional to the amount of time you set apart for the nourishment of your soul.

15. God's Xerox Copies
Text: Genesis 1: 26-7

Then God said, "Let us make man in our image, in our likeness, and let them rule over the fish of the sea and the birds of the air, over the livestock, over all the earth, and over all the creatures that moves along the ground." So God created man in his own image, in the image of God he created him; male and female he created them.

I belong to an organization called CITI Ministries, Inc. It is an organization of former Catholics, both priests and lay people who have left the Church for various reasons. In its December newsletter, I saw a notice that if any of us married priests wanted a personal website designed for free, please contact this number. So, I contacted the person and his name was Jim.

I provided him the information and he designed a website for me in a week.

I was so grateful to Jim for doing me such a favor. I wanted to show my appreciation but he wouldn't take any money. When I realized that he was a snowbird and was living in the Palm Beaches during the winter, I invited Jim and his wife for dinner to our house.

Jim is a retired systems engineer and his wife, Maria is a retired school teacher. Both of them have good pensions and they are living the life in a nice house near the sandy beaches of Florida.

We had a great dinner visit, talking about faith, family, Church, religion, bible and spirituality. Both of them are former Catholics but don't attend church anymore. I gave them a copy of my book and they were very curious about the title: *God is Plural.* They always thought that there was only one God and wondered why was I saying that God is Plural? Jim told me that he was confused about God.

I told them that for a lot of people, God is the biggest mystery.

Philosopher Rudolf Otto described God as *Mysterium Tremendum et Fascians* (*a tremendous and fascinating mystery*). Theologian Karl Rahner described God as *The Most Incomprehensible One.*

I too believe that God is a mystery. Instead of trying to understand this mystery from top down, **God as above us, beyond us and separate from us**, I am attempting to experience the mystery of God from the bottom up: **God as with us, within us and part of us.**

We had this top down understanding of God for 2000 years, and things haven't changed much. So I am taking a different approach.

I am not teaching anything new. It is as old as the book of Genesis, but most people have paid no attention to it. Describing the creation of the first humans, Genesis 1: 26 says: "Then God said: Let US make man in OUR image, after OUR likeness."

It does not say, Let ME make, but Let US make; it is PLURAL. The Hebrew word for God, *Elohim,* is PLURAL.
Then v. 27 says: "God created man in his image; in the divine image he created him; male and female he created THEM."

There you have it: the first humans, Adam and Eve are the original copies of the image and likeness of God. All humans, born into this world are xerox copies of God. And there are more than seven billion copies of God scattered around the globe in 212 plus countries. They come in all shapes, sizes, and colors imaginable. They come in different heights and weights, with abilities and disabilities. **They are as varied as the stars in the sky, and yet, as unique as their fingerprints!**

They all have one thing in common. Each one of them is imprinted with the image of God. And God, in his mysterious ways, has done something funny: he has scattered these images across the land. Our task is to find them. It is like a jigsaw puzzle. We have to find all those pieces of the puzzle and put them together. We don't have to literally see them with our eyes or touch them with our hands; **but we have to visualize them in our consciousness as one humanity, one divine tapestry of souls.**

When we do that, we will have a full picture of God. Perhaps that is what apostle John meant when he wrote: "No one has ever seen God; yet, if we love one another, God dwells in us, and his love is brought to perfection in us." (1Jn. 4:12)

Do you know why many people complain that they have not experienced God? Some people say "God does not exist," others say "God is dead," and others have just given up on God because it is just too complicated to understand God. They are talking about a God in the sky, a Supreme Being who is separate from us, **a being whose ego has to be inflated with our praises. A supernatural Being who needs to be manipulated with our prayers; someone who blesses the good and punishes the wicked. That is not God. That is a caricature of God.**

At the end of the dinner, Maria asked me: "So how do we see God's image in everyone, especially in people who irritate us, such as bad drivers or annoying neighbors?" I told her that she had to read the whole book!

So my dinner guests thanked us, gave us big hugs and went on their merry way. The next day, I got a nice e-mail from Jim thanking me for the sumptuous dinner and the warm hospitality.

I wrote back, once again expressing my gratitude for designing a free website and at the end, I wrote this: ***In my thinking, Maria and you are two more images of God consciously added to my collection, to make my image of God larger and more complete.***

And I was shocked by Jim's response the next day. He wrote: ***I never thought that Maria and I or ANYONE for that matter, could be images of God--although I have heard .hat phrase, "Made in God's image--my whole life...thinking about that brings a smile to my lips.***

I was shocked. Here is a 67 year old man, very intelligent and highly accomplished. He was a systems engineer at IBM for 29 years, and a senior engineer at Boeing for 15 years; married for 46 years with three children and ten grand children. He has traveled extensively and lived in several cities due to job related transfers. Born and raised Catholic, he was baptized as a baby, received first communion at age 10, was confirmed at 14, attended Mass faithfully every Sunday. He has listened to thousands of sermons, read the bible a few times, and read several spiritual books. We are not talking about an "average religious Joe" here.

And yet, and yet, he never thought or believed that he could be an image of God! You know what? If you don't consider yourself an image of God, you are unlikely to see people around you as images of God **because what you see out there, is a reflection of your inside!** Like philosopher Nietzhe, if you believe that "hell is other people," you are likely to see hell in front of you, and create hell for others. If you believe that other people are images of God, you are likely to treat them with respect and compassion.

The book of Genesis is not the only place where this message is stated. In the gospel of Luke, Jesus told his disciples: "Don't look for the Kingdom of God here and there, because the **Kingdom of God is within YOU!**" In John 10, when the Pharisees accused Jesus for claiming to be God, he turned around and asked them:

Is it not written in your law that you are gods? Apostle Paul asks the Corinthians: **Don't you know that you yourselves are God's temple and God's Spirit lives in you? God's temple is sacred and you are that temple.** (1Cor. 3:16)

Why didn't Jim who is a very religious man, a life-long Catholic, never thought he or his wife or anyone could be images of God? He admits to hearing it thousands of times. Why didn't he believe it? Why is it so hard to believe that, for many people?

Very often, we don't look for God in the people around us, because we have not been taught to do that. How are we expected to find God around us, when we are constantly told to look UP? The movie *Bruce Almighty* has an interesting scene. It is the movie where Jim Carrey gets the powers of God for a week. Jim is so frustrated that he cannot solve the problems of the world and so he runs back to God.

As God (played by Morgan Freeman) is climbing the stairs to the attic, a hapless Bruce asks God, looking up: "Are you leaving me? I need help."

"You are looking UP Bruce; that is your problem; that is everybody's problem."

I have patients who tell me, "I can't die, until the man upstairs decides." It is so hard to demolish the idea of God as a "man upstairs" that has been with us for centuries. But try it, and you will start experiencing life differently.

It is my strong conviction that unless and until I acknowledge, affirm and accept all the images of God scattered around the planet, we don't get a full picture of God.

MK Gandhi said it so beautifully: **"He who does not see God in the next person he meets, need look no further."**

Apostle John asks the same question: "How can you love God whom you have not seen, if you cannot love your brother whom you have seen?" (1John 4:21). So I take this image of God in everyone, very seriously.

Another reason we don't see God's image in people around us is, because, we are looking at them with the eyes of the flesh. Our physical eyes record only the superficial qualities of people. With these eyes we may see them as ugly, unfriendly, rude or inconsiderate. We may not like their color; we may not care about what they have to say or how they say it, especially if they have an accent. We may not approve of their sexual orientation.

But you know what? Underneath all that external stuff, there is a soul that is the same as yours; a soul that seeks love and approval, compassion and consideration; a soul that is exactly the same as yours; a soul that is a Xerox copy of God.

You need to slow down a moment to see that. Sages and mystics have called it as *seeing* with the 'inner eye' or the 'third eye.' You need to use your third eye, or the eye of the soul to see and connect with another soul. Always remember that what you see OUT there is a reflection of what is INSIDE of you, because, **we don't see things as they are, we see them as we are!**

When you experience yourself as an IMAGE of God, you will see IMAGES of God everywhere!

16. What God Wants
Text: Micah 6:8

God has told you, O mortal, what is good; and what does the Lord want of you but to do justice, and to love kindness, and to walk humbly with your God.

Today's sermon title is actually the title of a book by Neale Donald Walsh. He has written about 25 books and I have read almost all of them. His first book was called *Conversations with God,* which I read in the early 90s, and it changed my ideas about God, life and people. It made me a much happier and peaceful person.

What you *think* of God has great implications for how you live your life. You might say what we *tell* God (which is usually prayer) may have implications for life, but how does our *thinking* about God affect our daily lives? Our *theology* has a lot to do with our *sociology*; theology is what we think of God and sociology is what we think of society or people. They are intimately connected; one affects the other.

For example, if you think that God is this Powerful Supernatural Being who is separate from you, who needs to be praised and worshiped and obeyed, it is less likely to change your behavior because it is a fear-based and need-based understanding of God.

On the other hand, if you think that God is not SEPARATE from you, but is PART of you and everybody else, you are likely to feel empowered and not feel like a victim. You are likely to love and respect people around you, because God lives in them.
God has told you, O mortal, what is good; and what does the Lord want of you but to do justice, and to love kindness, and to walk humbly with your God.

Today's sermon title is actually the title of a book by Neale Donald Walsh. He has written about 25 books and I have read almost all of them. His first book was called *Conversations with God,* which I read in the early 90s, and it changed my ideas about God, life and people. It made me a much happier and peaceful person.

What you *think* of God has great implications for how you live your life. You might say what we *tell* God (which is usually prayer) may have implications for life, but how does our *thinking* about God affect our daily lives? Our *theology* has a lot to do with our *sociology*; theology is what we think of God and sociology is what we think of society or people. They are intimately connected; one affects the other.

For example, if you think that God is this Powerful Supernatural Being who is separate from you, who needs to be praised and worshiped and obeyed, it is less likely to change your behavior because it is a fear-based and need-based understanding of God.

On the other hand, if you think that God is not SEPARATE from you, but is PART of you and everybody else, you are likely to feel empowered and not feel like a victim. You are likely to love and respect people around you, because God lives in them.

Most people think that a conversation *with* God is impossible. We can talk *to* God but not *with* God, because for most people their relationship with God is not a partnership, but a servant-master relationship. There is a big difference. We talk to God all the time. It is called prayer. We don't usually have a dialogue with God, we only have monologues. We are doing all the talking, and we don't hear God talking to us.

Many people don't really believe that God talks to humans today. "God talked to Moses 3000 years ago and it is all written down in the bible; just read it," they would say. I cannot believe that God stopped talking 3000 years ago.

What kind of God is that, who only talked in the past, to a select group of people and He expects that people to write it all down, in a language we don't read or write and scholars have to translate all that for us?

Does God talk to us today? The common answer is: "He might talk to holy people, but not to me, because I am unworthy to be spoken to by God." So, many people don't expect to hear from God, and as a result, they don't listen or don't pay attention.

It is very unfortunate. What is sad is that even some pastors don't believe it. There is an elder at my church who is 90 years old. She is still fairly healthy. Theologically, she is conservative. But she read the first volume of *Conversations with God*. She was so excited about the new ideas about God in that book. She told the pastor what a great book it was and the pastor just brushed her off. He said: "God does not come for a chat."

This pastor continues to see God as a Supreme Being separate from us who is too big to talk to us. According to Neale Donald Walsch, *If someone says that he talks to God every day, he will be called pious. But if someone says that God talks to him every day, he will be called crazy; what is really crazy is thinking that God stopped talking 3000 years ago.*
The question today is not whether God talks to us, but who listens?

So what does God want from us? I Googled that question and I was not happy with the answers I found. The gist of the answers is that God wants us to be obedient to him; that God wants us to do His will; that God wants us to praise and worship him; that

God wants us to pray to him for our needs and ask forgiveness for our sins.

I didn't like any of those answers because the underlying thinking behind all those answers is that God is separate from us; that God is out there, up there, and it is a *He;* and He needs something from us in return for creating us.

Since I was not happy with the answers I found on *Google*, I posted that question on my Facebook page. I have 192 friends on Facebook. I expected many to answer that question. But surprisingly, I got only two answers and both were from my pastor friends.

One friend wrote: "Here are the buzz words I usually hear in church, almost any church on any given Sunday...blood, sin, repent, give. It may not be what God wants, but that is what many people are led to think."

My second pastor-friend wrote: "There is a philosophical answer and a biblical answer. The philosophical answer is that God wants nothing, because God lacks nothing; He is perfect. For the biblical answer, he quoted from the book of *Micah* which is an obscure book in the Old Testament. It is rarely read in churches. This is what Micah 6:8 says: "God has told you, O mortal, what is good; and what does the Lord want of you but to do justice, and to love kindness, and to walk humbly with your God."

I like that answer. But I don't like the way it is explained. It sounds like a requirement and a command; that God who is separate from you, wants you to do these things: do justice, love kindness and humbly walk with God.

Do justice. That is too general; Love kindness, that is too vague, and walk humbly with God: how do you do that on a daily basis? What does that involve?

So, I am going to give you the answer from the book, *What God Wants* by Neale Donald Walsch. I like his answer. I began reading this book wanting to find the answer to that gigantic question. What does God really want from us His children?

As I began reading, the author promised the answer in chapter 13. In the last paragraph of the 12th chapter he writes: "So don't be surprised if you are resistant to the breathtaking revelation on the next page. Yet now is the time for change—and the next chapter could be much more than a new chapter in this book. It could be a new chapter in your life."

And with great anticipation, I turned the page to chapter 13. Guess what I found? Six blank pages!

God wants nothing from us; absolutely nothing. It is so hard for us to get our mind around that but that is the truth.

Let me try to explain that in the context of Fathers Day. We are told by Jesus that God is our father. The most famous prayer of all times is called the *Our Father*. So, there is no argument; God is our father. So, what does God our father want from us his children?

I like to reflect on this based on my experience as a father. Those who are fathers here please think in terms of your fatherhood. I have two sons, Johnny and Tommy. Johnny is 19 and he is autistic. Tommy is 17 and he is "normal" whatever that means for a teenager. Because of his autism, Johnny is unlikely to achieve the basic goals of life such as college graduation, a high paying job or marriage. So I will use Tommy as an example.

As his father, what do I want from Tommy? I want you keep the image of God as father in your mind simultaneously. I want him to study hard, have dreams, set goals, and have the discipline to achieve them. I want him to be happy and succeed in life. Even though I use the word *want*, I don't want any of that for myself, I want it for him. I want him to do all that independently of me. I don't want him to be subservient or dependent on me.

Consider a different scenario. Suppose my son does not go to school regularly, sleeps all day, uses drugs and gets involved with the wrong crowd. I will be very unhappy and disappointed. When he is home, he is nice to me. He tells me what a wonderful dad I am. He asks me for money all the time, because he doesn't have a job. I will be disgusted with that scenario. I want him to grow up and leave home and make a life for himself. Even if he never calls me or visits me, but if I know he is living a happy and successful life somewhere, I will be delighted.

Last weekend, Judy and I attended a graduation party for someone we had known for twenty years. When we first met them, Michael was 3 years old. We had seen him periodically during his school years, but hadn't seen him since he went to University of Florida in Gainesville. I could not take my eyes off of this handsome young man who is now 23 and just graduated from law school with *summa cum laude.*

I was fascinated by the demeanor and behavior of Michael's father, John. John was always a low key, subdued person. But this night was different. He was talking proudly about his son, what a great young man he had become and how hard he worked to become a lawyer. He has a full scholarship to study tax law at NYU. John was gushing through all the openings on his face. As a father, he was on the top of the world, because his son had grown up to be a fine young man, independent, educated and self-sufficient. All that happiness and pride is not because John wants anything from his son for himself. He wants Michael to succeed for Michael's sake, not for his sake. And I don't think Michael worked hard and became a lawyer to please his dad or because his dad wanted that from him. Michael did it for himself.

Our relationship to God our father should be something like that.

God is delighted when we function independently of God. That does not mean away from God or devoid of God, but living our lives by using the power that God has already given us by creating us in his image.

Instead of feeling like weak sinners, God wants us to feel empowered by His presence within us; God wants us to be His equal partner not a lowly servant; God wants us to be His co-creator not an unworthy creature; God does not want us to live our lives tainted by original sin, but blessed by His abundant grace.

In short, God wants us to grow up. God wants none of this for his glorification, but for us to have a glorious life.

Somebody once asked me a question: "Aren't we created to glorify God?" Of course we are. But what does glorifying God mean? Does it mean repeating phrases like "We have an awesome God" or "Our God is greater than your God" or singing praises to a Supreme Being beyond the clouds? I will repeat the answer given by St. Ireneus, centuries ago. *Homo Vivens, Gloria Dei.* **God's glory is a human being fully alive.**

And when we are "fully alive," we will do justice, love kindness, and walk humbly with God."

17. From Limping to Dancing
Text: Matthew 9: 1-8

Jesus stepped into a boat, crossed over, and came to his own town. Some men brought to him a paralytic, lying on a mat. When Jesus saw their faith, he said to the paralytic, "Take heart, son; your sins are forgiven." At this, some of the teachers of the law said to themselves, "This fellow is blaspheming!" Knowing their thoughts, Jesus said, "Why do you entertain evil thoughts in your hearts? Which is easier to say, 'Your sins are forgiven,' or to say, 'Get up and walk'? But so that you may know that the Son of Man has authority on earth to forgive sins..." Then he said to the paralytic, "Get up, take your mat and go home." And the man got up and went home. When the crowd saw this, they were filled with awe; and they praised God, who had given such authority to men.

Everybody knows what limping means. Either you have limped at some point in your life or you have seen someone limping. The last time I saw someone limping was during a visit to a patient who had foot surgery, limping from his bedroom to the bathroom. Last week I visited a neighbor who had knee surgery and he was limping around his house, using crutches.

You cannot go dancing if you are limping; it won't look pretty or feel comfortable. You need healthy legs to do the dance movements and enjoy the experience.

If you see somebody limping, you are likely to ask: "What is wrong?" because we know that a healthy person is not supposed to limp.

So far, I was talking about physical limping. But I think that for a lot of people, limping is a metaphor for life. A large majority of people in this world are actually limping through life. Some of them use crutches, like drug, alcohol, coffee, cigarettes and other mood altering substances. Others may not use obvious crutches, but they are limping nonetheless.

Why are so many people limping through life? The obvious answer is they are carrying heavy burdens. That is true. If you are carrying heavy things on your shoulders, you will limp.

What are some of these burdens? Physical illness, not having enough money to pay bills, lack of good relationship with a spouse or family members, unemployment, recession and threat of terrorism are some of the burdens that make people limp through life, and there are plenty others.

So what do we do? Just carry them, grumbling under our breath, and limping all the way? Or is there a way to dance through life, in spite of all the burdens we have to carry?

Let's face it; some of the burdens are inevitable, such as a terminal illness, taxes and death. If you get cancer, there is not a whole lot you can do about it, except getting chemo or radiation, which can be burdensome in themselves. You might limp a little, but if you really trust the words of Jesus, "Come to me those who are tired and heavy burdened, and I will comfort you," you will do better. Or the other promise of Jesus, "Let not your hearts be troubled; trust in me and trust in my Father." If you remember those words and take them into our heart, you might dance with a little limp.

After making allowance for the inevitable wounds of life that make us limp, I still feel that majority of the wounds that cause our limping are self-inflicted.

I am reminded of the story of a family I visited last week. Rhoda is a 91 year old woman who is a hospice patient on my team. She is Jewish. Her son, who is the primary care giver and Power of Attorney, had called the office and told my manager that a visit from the chaplain would not be necessary, because they are not religious; besides, they preferred a rabbi.

I did not get that memo on time. So, Monday morning I went to work as usual. I went to the Assisted Living Facility where we have almost twenty patients in the same building.

I knocked at Rhoda's door. There was a man sitting on the couch who said to me: "You must be Chaplain Paul; you could have saved a trip, because I had told your manager that a chaplain visit was not needed; besides, my mom wants to be quiet; she does not want to be seen lying helplessly."

And I said, "I can understand that and I respect that, but since I am here, can I chat with you a little." He told me his name was Ben and he was the oldest of Rhoda's five children.

I sat down, and during the two and a half hours of conversation, I had the privilege to peek into the pathological plight of a family limping through life, for no good reason. Ben described his family as totally dysfunctional, filled with jealousy, hatred and bitterness towards each other.

Three years ago, when his mother was approaching that stage of life when she was no longer able to take care of her affairs, she appointed Ben as her Power of Attorney. That infuriated the other four siblings, his two brothers, Melvin and Brad, and two sisters, Linda and Joan. And they reportedly began 'ganging up' on him. Nasty emails and phone calls were exchanged between the siblings. Ben was accused of causing a heart attack for one of his sisters who apparently had to call 911 because she was so stressed out by the drama happening in their lives.

Ben played two voice mail messages from his sister calling him a liar and telling him that God will punish him in hell for what he was doing to the family.

Two weeks ago, the younger son, Melvin visited his mother when Ben was away, and he wanted to take his mother to an attorney to make him the POA. His mother was furious. She did not want to be dragged from her death bed to an attorney's office.

The next day, she told Ben that she did not want to die seeing her children fighting. So he sent an email to his siblings inviting them to come for a reconciliation gathering. No one responded to that email.

This family is definitely not dancing through life; they are limping badly. There is so much anger, jealousy, discontentment and pure animosity; their dying mother feels helpless and wonders what she did wrong to deserve this at the end!

This is just one example of thousands of individuals and families that are limping through life out there, totally missing out on the fullness of life that Jesus promised. Why?

I was reading a book called *Dance* by Oriah Mountain Dreamer. The author asks:

What if the question is not, *"Why am I so infrequently the person I really want to be?"* But rather, **"Why do I so infrequently want to be the person I really AM?"**

Let me simplify: Why don't you show me who you are, rather than try to get something from somewhere to show me? Who you are is good and worthy.

In other words, instead of trying so hard to BECOME something, like more patient, more loving, more joyful or more compassionate, why don't you just BE who you ALREADY ARE: patient, loving, joyful, and compassionate. That is what you are; that is what you are created to be because, God does not create junk.

God created you with all those qualities; you messed it up. God created you in His image and likeness; God created you as temples of the Holy Spirit. You are not aware of it, or you don't believe it, and so, you limp through life in this vale of tears, barely making it.

Who you are is enough. We live our deepest desires of our soul not by intending to CHANGE who we are but by intending to BE who we are. In other words, you don't have to wait for something to happen; you don't have to make something happen; all you have to do is awaken to what is already happening in your life.

If our intention is to BE who we are, to fully manifest who we really are -*the image of God*- then we will make choices to expand that image. On the other hand, if we are trying to change, that means we think we are flawed and we need to try so hard to change.

The author says that "this lack of faith in who we are is embedded in the bones of the culture we have created. We are surrounded by the assumption of our inadequacy; we are constantly told that we are sinners, born with 'original sin' because that is what we see around us and within us all the time; sinful behaviors and signs of weakness. We rarely bother to check deep inside of us."

The marketplace is flooded with books, tapes and teachers telling us how to change ourselves into something other than what we are implying that who we are isn't enough.

Stop trying so hard. How many resolutions have you made but failed miserably in keeping them? How many Lenten seasons have you observed, trying so hard to change your life and still not achieved your goals?

Oriah Mountain Dreamer says that many people are not dancing through life because, *Very often, we live merely in the NEIGHBORHOOD of our SELF. We are limping through the periphery of our self, paying attention to superficial stuff. We rarely go deep into our inner being to see what a beautiful soul God has created and placed inside of us: a spark of God, waiting to be ignited. We drive around the neighborhood of our soul and no wonder, we are just wandering or getting lost; we are not getting home or feeling at home.*

Lent is often referred to as a "time of renewal." I prefer "a period of recovery." In *A New Earth: Awakening to Your Life's Purpose*, Eckhart Tolle says: *You do not become good by trying to be good, but by finding the goodness that is already within you, and allowing that goodness to emerge. But it can only emerge if something fundamentally changes in your state of consciousness.*

That is exactly what I am talking about; you must change your consciousness from "I am a sinful being" to "I am a spiritual being."

That is why I place before you on this first Sunday of Lent, the story of the paralytic. Here is a man who could not move and is brought before Jesus, being carried by his friends. He could not even limp, he was paralyzed. See what happened to him in the presence of Jesus. Jesus forgives his sins, and his paralysis is healed.

Look at it closely. Here is a man with physical paralysis. But Jesus does not do a physical exam. He does not check out his legs to see if he has enough muscle strength to stand up. Jesus does not check and see if had a stroke or a heart attack that may have caused his paralysis. Jesus is not concerned about the physical side of his problem at all.

Instead, Jesus says just one thing: "Take heart son, your sins are forgiven." Jesus was talking to the inner being of the man; he was not talking to the body of the man; He was talking to his soul. If your soul is cleaned up, your body too will clean up and become healthy.

We may be walking straight without physical limping, but we may be limping due to spiritual paralysis caused by fear, anxiety, prejudice, unforgiving attitude or lack of compassion. During this Lent, Jesus offers us an opportunity for healing.

One of the most valuable Lenten disciplines is faithfulness to daily prayer. Find some time every day to quiet your mind and heart, to recover a state of consciousness in which you are once again aware of being united with the Holy One.

You don't have to say any prayers. Read a passage from the gospel or any inspiring book and sit still. It is very hard. Try it for 15 minutes for 40 days, and you will experience a new sense of calm and peace happening inside. We will learn again who we are, why we are, and restore what is of most value to our life. In other words, we will once again learn how to dance through life.

18. The Fifth Gospel
Text: 2Corinthians 3: 1-3

Are we beginning to commend ourselves again? Or do we need, like some people, letters of recommendation to you or from you? You yourselves are our letter, written on your hearts, known and read by everybody. You show that you are a letter from Christ, the result of our ministry, written not with ink but with the Spirit of the living God, not on tablets of stone but on tablets of human hearts.

We all know the four gospels: Mathew, Mark, Luke and John. Is there a fifth gospel? There is the gospel of Thomas and gospel of Judas and several other gospels, but they are not approved by the Church or included in the Official Cannon of the bible.

But there is a fifth gospel. It is not a gospel printed on the pages of a book; it is not a gospel that you can pick up in your hands and read. No, you cannot download it on your *Nook* or *Kindle*.

It is a living gospel that walks and talks and moves; it is a gospel that you can look straight up and read; it is none other than you. The fifth gospel is YOU! We are a gospel to each other.

When we hear the word 'gospel' we usually think of a book. But the word gospel simply means "good news."

So I encourage you to change your thinking today. Instead of thinking about the four books in the Bible exclusively as gospels, I want you to think of yourselves as gospels. That is what Apostle Paul wants you to do today.

In today's text, Paul says: *You are my letter, known and read by all people, written on your hearts. Clearly, you are a letter of Christ which I have delivered. A letter not written with ink, but by the Spirit of the living God. Not on tablets of stone, but of tablets of flesh in the heart.*

I get goose bumps when I read those words, because Paul is talking about us. So, let us study the characteristics of this letter. First of all, **you are a letter known and read by everybody.**

There is so much illiteracy in the world; even among the literate, only very few people read books. But Paul says, even those who don't read traditional books, read you.

We read people and people read us all the time. It is a common phenomenon. Those of you who have known each other for a long time, you have read each other already. It is like a book you have finished reading. You know what it contains.

When you meet a person for the very first time, you do an initial reading; it is like checking out the front and back covers of a book. We read each person differently, depending on what is written on them.

I read two people very differently last week. My car needed some transmission work. So I stopped by an Aamco shop in Coral Springs. The guy at the front desk was on his computer, totally oblivious, not even bothering to acknowledge that a customer had walked in. I stood there looking at him, trying to get his attention, but had no luck; he was not a pleasant letter to read and I walked out.

I went into another Aamco shop in a different town near my office and the man was also on his computer; but he motioned to me to take a seat and said: "I will be with you in a moment." When he was done, he came out, shook my hand, introduced himself and asked how he could help. I told him about the problem my car had; he gave me an estimate and the work was done in an hour, and I was on my way. He was a pleasant letter to read.

So remember Paul's first advice: You are a letter read by every one around you.

Secondly, Paul says, **you are a letter of Christ, written by the Spirit of the living God**. Think about that for a moment. You are not a piece of junk mail callously tossed in your mailbox by an overworked mailman; you are a letter of Christ written and delivered by God.

We know what happens to junk mail; they get tossed out. I don't know how you deal with them. When I pick up my mail, I pass through the garage and stand over the trash can; every piece of junk mail is tossed in. I don't even take them inside the house. But letters from family and friends are taken inside, opened, read, loved and appreciated. There is a feeling of warmth and love when you read letters from family and friends.

Letters are so important in our lives. It is letters and cards from family and friends that sustain the elderly population. If you watch the elderly people in those high rise condos on the beach, you will see that the one person they are waiting for every day is the mail man.

I visit several ALFs to see hospice patients. I see residents coming down to the area of the mail boxes, some days, several times to see if the mail man had come. And around three o'clock, there is a stampede around the mail boxes, wheel chairs and walkers hitting each other; they are eager to get their mail. They are hoping that somebody sent them a card or a letter.

Thirty years ago when I was studying in Canada, there was no email or phone communication for me. My connection to family and friends in India was entirely through snail mail. There was a clipboard in the rectory office with my name on it. Every day, when I returned from school my eyes would always fall first on that clipboard. If I had a letter from India, it would be on that clip. When I saw it from a few feet away, my heart would fill up with joy.

Even today, I wait for the mailman. Letters rarely come by snail mail anymore, but I still wait; of course I check may e-mail every day. It is always good to receive letters, snail-mail or e-mail.

Do people in your life wait eagerly for you? Are they happy to see you when you go home?" Are your colleagues happy to see you when you get to the office? Are you a letter that contains good news? Or a piece of junk mail that people would rather avoid or discard?

Thirdly, Paul says that we are **letters written not on tablets of stone but on tablets of human hearts.** What are the messages that are written on your heart? Are they messages of love, compassion and joy, or are they messages of anger, prejudice and judgment? You don't have to say anything using words; if those negative messages are written on your heart, people can read them.

In psychology 101, I was taught that 65 per cent of our communication is through non-verbal language. So it is not enough to just guard our tongue; it is important to watch our demeanor too, because people are reading us all the time, whether we know it or not. That is why **years later, people will forget what you told them or what you did for them,** *but they will never forget how you made them feel.*

And the feeling they get is received not by listening to you as a speaker, but by reading you as a letter.

Apostle Paul reminds us that we are living letters. In 2Cor. 2:14, Paul says that "Christ employs us to diffuse the fragrance of his knowledge everywhere." How do we diffuse or spread the fragrance of his knowledge? How do we make Christ known to others?

I know in the gospel of Mathew, there is this great commission to go and preach the good news. Jesus told his disciples to preach the good news around the world. But traditional ways of preaching the good news are becoming increasingly hard these days. In the fifties, missionaries from the West used to come to India and preach the gospel and convert Hindus. Actually Christianity started in India due to the preaching of St. Thomas in the first century, and Francis Xavier in the 19th century.

But in India today, due to an anti-conversion bill passed by the parliament, it is against the law of the land to overtly convert people from one religion to another. Missionaries can't do their traditional preaching any more. Few years ago, there was a story about two women from a church in Texas who went to Saudi Arabia, dressed up as Muslims and preached the gospel. They were arrested, imprisoned and later, deported.

So, overt preaching is out, but there is something all Christians can do whether they are in America, India or Saudi Arabia. And that is to let people read the living letters that they are, and help others find Christ in that process. This was so effective in the case of the disciples of Francis of Assisi. When he sent out his disciples into different parts of the world, Francis of Assisi told them to **preach always and use words, if necessary.**

A few verses above in today's reading, Paul says something even more beautiful. He says that **we are to God the aroma of Christ. Yes, we are the aroma of Christ.**

Once a month, I go to *Massage Envy* for a massage. I love going there, because as soon as you walk in, there is a very pleasant aroma. Last month, I got an aroma therapy session, with scented candle and soothing oil. It was just so beautifully pleasant. When I walk into nursing homes to visit my patients, the aroma there is not that pleasant.

I am sure you have experienced both aroma and unpleasant smell in your life. When I hug them, some people say: "You smell so good." They are referring to my after shave lotion. I wish it was the aroma of Christ!

The aroma of Christ is not contained in a bottle that you can buy at Victoria Secret. The aroma of Christ is contained in your heart as compassionate love, gentle peace, goodness, kindness and joy.

We are the aroma of Christ in a world that is stinking with the smell of hate and prejudice and restlessness. We are a letter of good news in a world that is filled with the junk mail of division and disunity.

If we fail to be good news to the people around us and fail to spread the aroma of Christ around us, we have failed as disciples of Jesus.

19. Living Inside Out
Text: Mark 4: 35-41

That day when evening came, he said to his disciples, "Let us go over to the other side." Leaving the crowd behind, they took him along, just as he was, in the boat. There were also other boats with him. A furious squall came up, and the waves broke over the boat, so that it was nearly swamped. Jesus was in the stern, sleeping on a cushion. The disciples woke him and said to him, "Teacher, don't you care if we drown?"

He got up, rebuked the wind and said to the waves, "Quiet! Be still!" then the wind died down and it was completely calm. He said to his disciples, "Why are you so afraid? Do you still have no faith?" They were terrified and asked each other, "Who is this, even the wind and the waves obey him!"

A woman in a supermarket is following a grandfather and his 3 year-old grandson. The grandson is behaving very badly. It's obvious to her that he has his hands full with the child screaming for candy in the sweets aisle, for biscuits and fruits, cereal and cookies in the other aisles.

Meanwhile, Gramps is working his way around, saying in a controlled voice, "Easy William, we won't be long... easy boy."

Another outburst and she hears the granddad calmly say, "It's okay William, just a couple more minutes and we'll be out of here; hang in there, boy."

At the checkout, the little terror is throwing items out of the cart, and Gramps says again in a controlled voice, "William, William, relax buddy, don't get upset. We'll be home in five minutes; stay cool, William."

Very impressed, the woman goes outside where the grandfather is loading his groceries and the boy into the car.

She said to the elderly gentleman, "It's none of my business, but you were amazing in there. I don't know how you did it. That whole time, you kept your composure, and no matter how loud and disruptive he got, you just calmly kept saying, things would be okay. William is very lucky to have you as his grandpa."

"Thanks lady," said the grandfather, "but *I'm William*...the little bastard's name is Steve."

It is a cute little story. Today's sermon is about the message of that story. What is the message? Someone said the message is: "Don't go grocery shopping with little ones." Or the story shows how undisciplined our kids are. No; that is not the message I want to focus on. For me, it is a great story about living our lives inside out, rather than outside in.

You can live your life two ways: *Outside in* or *Inside out.* Outside in, means you are affected by everything that happens *around* or *outside* of you. Few weeks ago, I was watching TV with a group of people when the *Casey Anthony* murder trial verdict came down on July 5th. Some people were pounding the table, cursing the TV and they were so bent out of shape that I could see their veins popping. Or take the case of thousands of hockey fans in Vancouver. When their team lost, they took it to the streets, vandalizing cars and shops, and getting arrested.

Their emotions were controlled by outside events. **When you live your life outside in, you have no control over your life. You don't make any choices; your life is determined by the choices and behaviors of others. You are a victim of circumstances; you are like a cork in the ocean tossing around with no purpose or direction, totally at the mercy of wind.**

I saw a good example of such a life on a bumper sticker the other day. *I am happy today; don't ruin it.*

What it means is that if someone happens to cut him off or honk at him, his happiness will be ruined. His happiness is dependent upon the behaviors of other drivers. Imagine that for a moment. Your happiness is dependent upon how other people behave. Good luck with that. Why would you want to give control of your emotions and feelings to other people whom you don't even know most of the time? Why would you want to be a cork in the ocean of life?

We have no control over how other people are going to behave. We have no control as to what is going to happen to us or to our family tomorrow. In other words, we have very little control over what happens outside of our lives.

If my happiness and peace is dependent upon other people, I should be prepared to be miserable most of the time, because I can't count on others to make me happy. That is giving control of my life to others; that is living my life outside in.

This is true for a lot of marriages. The husband expects the wife to make him happy and vice versa. You have heard the saying that marriage is 50-50. I don't believe in that formula, which implies that unless the other spouse comes up with the 50 percent, the marriage is never a 100 percent. That is a lot of pressure. And we know that humans always fall short. I believe that marriage should be built on a 100-100 formula. Each partner should shoot for a hundred, so that even if one fails some days, you still have a hundred.

That is why early on, I made a choice in my marriage. I try to live by the following philosophy: **Demand nothing, expect something and hope for everything**. Because, when you demand love from your spouse, and let us say you get it, it is not love anymore; it is given grudgingly. When you demand that the house be clean and dinner be ready when you get home, you are expecting your spouse to meet your demand; your happiness depends on your spouse meeting your expectations; and if the expectations are not met, there is pouting, maybe cursing, and sometimes breaking stuff resulting in tension and unhappiness. That is an example of living your life outside in. You let outside circumstances determine your state of mind.

The better way to live is to live your life inside out. That is, you are taking charge of your peace and happiness by being in charge. You control your thoughts and feelings from inside. Every thought you have has an energy that will either strengthen or weaken you. If you think the world is a hostile place, you are more than likely to experience it that way; if on the other hand, you think that the world is by far a friendly place, you are likely to experience that.

Fr. Anthony D'Mello, in his book *One Minute Wisdom*, has a student ask this question:

"Why is everyone here so happy except me? And the master replied: "Because they have learned to see goodness and beauty everywhere."

"Why don't I see goodness and beauty everywhere" asked the student and the master said: "Because, you cannot see outside of you what you fail to see inside." That is what I mean by living your life inside out. You determine the impact of what is happening outside, based on what is inside you.

Let me tell you a story to explain this: There was a farmer living in the villages of Burma with his wife and only son. He had a horse which was his precious possession. One day, the horse ran away into the forest. The neighbors came by and said to the farmer: *It is bad luck for you.* And the farmer said: *Good luck back luck God knows.* The next day, the horse returned to the farm, bringing along a few wild horses. The neighbors came back and said: *It is good luck for you now* and the farmer said: *Good luck, bad luck, God knows.*

The following day, the son while training one of the wild horses fell off and broke his leg and the neighbors came by and said: *It is bad luck for you* and the man said: *Good luck bad luck God knows.*

A few days later a war broke out with the neighboring country and all the able bodied youth were drafted, but the young man was spared because his leg was broken. The neighbors returned to say: *You are a lucky man* and the father said again: *Good luck, bad luck, God knows.*

This farmer is a good example of living his life inside out. There were several outside events that could have thrown his life off balance. Each incident had the potential for taking his life on a roller coaster ride of ecstasy and emptiness. He didn't succumb to either; his neighbors got all excited and even tried their best to drag him with them, but he refused. **He saw the big picture; he had the presence of mind to see life as a series of ups and downs; his peace of mind was not determined by the happenings around him, but the processing that happened inside, and so he remained calm and peaceful throughout.**

Wayne Dyer has a saying that beautifully captures the essence of living your life inside out: **You feel good not because the world is right, but your world is right because you feel good.**

How do you feel good when so much of the world around you is not right? Internationally, there is poverty and terrorism. Nationally, there is unemployment and foreclosures. Personally, there are health issues, financial problems, relationship issues. Think of all the issues you are dealing with on a personal level.

The world around us is not very pretty; in fact, it could be very sad and frightening at times. What do we do?

Today's gospel story will help us navigate this world. Let us look at the story. Jesus and his disciples had a long day; they wanted some time away from the demanding crowd. So they decided to go to the other side of the lake of Galilee on a boat. Now I want you to imagine this scene as vividly as possible.

They are on a little boat. Don't think of the cruise ship, *Oasis of the Seas* owned by Carnival Cruise lines. It is a small wooden boat that can carry about ten people and it will toss like a cork if there are waves. And there were waves. The story says, "A furious squall came up and the waves broke over the boat so that it was nearly swamped." If you have ever been in a boat like that, it can be a frightening experience. (I don't know why the disciples were so frightened; most of them were former fishermen and they must have come across similar experiences before; but that is another discussion).

So they woke up Jesus and said: "Teacher, don't you care if we drown?"

Now the disciples in this story are perfect examples of people living their lives *outside in*. When they saw the storm and the squall, they got scared. Their focus was on the storm. They were looking at the waves coming into the boat. Their attention was totally focused on the external events happening around them. No wonder they were afraid, because what they saw outside was indeed scary. And they began to shake in their pants, or shall I say, their tunics.

Now, Jesus in this story is a perfect example of a person living his life *inside out*. He too, like the disciples, was surrounded by squall. He is in the same boat with them, no pun intended; it is tossing and turning, but imagine that scene where Jesus is sleeping at the stern with a cushion. The events around him don't affect his peace; he is not afraid; He had strong faith in his Father and that sustained him throughout the storm.

After calming the storm, Jesus asked his disciples about their faith; he told them that they were afraid of the external storm, because they did not draw from their internal faith. This happens to us every time we live our lives outside in.

Jesus was calm right in the middle of the storm because of his inner life. Jesus cultivated a deep inner life right from the beginning. He fasted and prayed for forty days and forty nights before he made the first public appearance. During his ministry, we always see Jesus going away from the crowd, into the quiet, to pray. The gospels don't say how Jesus prayed, but I believe he was constantly reflecting and meditating in silence.

Do you have an inner life? What is inner life anyway? It is a life of reflection, insight and vision. Having eye sight does not mean you have insight; attending church every Sunday by itself is not a guarantee of inner life; reading the bible and believing it literally may not necessarily make you a person of inner life.

Inner life is much deeper than all that. It takes effort to practice and cultivate it. In requires being able to sit still for a few minutes each day to deeply reflect on the meaning of life and the working of God in our lives. It requires reading spiritual books; it demands getting off the fast lane of life.

Inner life is about having a wider perspective on life; inner life enables you to see the big picture; inner life makes you love unconditionally and forgive easily; inner life makes you not sweat the small stuff; inner life helps you to live in the moment and not be anxious about tomorrow.

A person with an inner life does not get overly excited about superficial stuff. Inner life will give you inner peace, the peace that passeth understanding, the peace that the world can neither give nor takes away.

As I said, it takes effort and time to cultivate an inner life; but once you have it, you would wonder how you lived so long without it. It is like finding a pearl of great value that Jesus talks about.

If you can find ten minutes a day in the morning and ten minutes at night to sit still and practice meditation, you will start seeing changes in your life within a week. Your life will be guided by the promptings and priorities of the soul regardless of what happens outside of you. Then you will start experiencing the *abundant life* that Jesus promised!

20. Everyday Miracles
Text: John 9: 35-41

Jesus heard that they had thrown him out and when he found him, he said, "Do you believe in the Son of Man?" "Who is he, sir?" the man asked. "Tell me so that I may believe in him." Jesus said, "You have now seen him; in fact, he is the one speaking with you." Then the man said, "Lord, I believe," and he worshipped him.

Jesus said, "For judgment I have come into this world, so that the blind will see and those who see will become blind." Some Pharisees who were with him heard him say this and asked, "What? Are we blind too?" Jesus said, "If you were blind, you would not be guilty of sin; but now that you claim you can see, your guilt remains.

Have any of you experienced any miracles lately? When we hear the word 'miracle,' what comes to mind is something that is out of the ordinary, an event or an experience that is off the chart. Webster's Dictionary defines miracle as: "An extremely outstanding or unusual event, or an extraordinary event manifesting divine intervention in human affairs."

As Christians, when we hear the word miracle, we usually think about the miracles of Jesus. There are about 17 miracles listed in the four gospels. According to John, the first miracle was the turning of water into wine during a wedding in Cana. Then there is Jesus walking on the water, Jesus multiplying fish and loaves and feeding 5000, Jesus healing the lepers, Jesus raising the daughter of Jairus, etc.

Moving away from biblical times, we have learned to recognize miracles these days; for example when someone is rescued from a burning building, we will say that was a "miraculous" rescue. Or when someone is healed of cancer, we will say that was a "miraculous" cure. Somebody described the tallest building in Dubai as a modern day miracle. Of course we have the "Seven wonders of the world."

I invite you today to move away from the notion that for something to be miraculous, it has to be off the chart, or out of the ordinary. I would like to show you today how to see the miraculous and the mysterious in the simple, trivial, run of the mill, ordinary events and experiences of our lives. It is a wonderful way to live.

This sermon was inspired by a sign in a church: *Expect a Miracle*. That sign is based on the dictionary definition of miracle as "an extraordinary event manifesting divine intervention." Expect means look for, hope for or wait for something to happen. And we will be happy with *a* miracle.

But, don't just "expect" *a* miracle, sometime in the future, but experience the many miracles that are happening right within you and around you all the time. We don't see them because, we are sleepwalking through life; we don't experience them because we are not awake.

We can be physically awake and mentally asleep. Our eyes may be open but we may not be seeing. Looking and seeing are entirely different things. When you look towards the east in the morning, it seems like the sun is rising above the ocean. It seems very real. While you look at that "rising sun," if you can SEE that the sun is not rising but the earth is moving, then you are really SEEING.

Or, when you look at a man who is holding a sign asking for money, and you say to yourself: "He must be a drug addict" you are just looking at his outside. If you were to say, "He could be Jesus" then you are SEEING.

It is called seeing with the "third eye." It takes some practice to see with the third eye, but once you get a taste of it, you will be amazed what a difference it makes. You will ask yourself, "How did I live so long without using my third eye?" It is like getting prescription glasses for the first time. You start seeing the world around you more clearly and vividly.

In addition to our two physical eyes, we have a third eye. But first, you have to believe that you have it and secondly, you have to practice seeing through it. Your life and the world will never be the same again.

I have been using my third eye for a while now, and life has been *fantasticulous*. That is a word I just made up. It is a combination of fantastic and fabulous. Did you know that you can make up words, and if enough people use it, it will be added to the Webster's Dictionary?

This year, they added 150 new words. One of them is *tweet*. Another word they added this year is *bromance*. It means a non-sexual close friendship between men. I belong to a men's group. We are five of us, very close, and we have been meeting twice a month for years; we don't drink, smoke or talk about sports. We discuss spiritual topics that men usually don't talk about.

Until this year, we did not have an acceptable word to describe our gathering. Somebody labeled us "five straight guys acting like gays." Now we have a word to describe our experience: *bromance*. Some other words that were added this year are *helicopter parent, boomerang children,* and *fist bump*.

But I digress; coming back to seeing with the third eye.

The origins of the third eye are in Hinduism. In the Hindu Trinity, the three gods are *Brahma, Vishnu* and *Shiva*. Yes, they have a

Trinity like ours, Father, Son and the Holy Spirit. The third person of the Hindu Trinity, *Shiva*, the Destroyer, is depicted with a third eye in the center of his forehead. Usually closed, the third eye is supposed to have appeared when his consort, *Parvati,* playfully covered both his eyes with her hands as *Shiva* sat rapt in meditation. Immediately the universe was plunged in darkness. Chaos reigned supreme.

Shiva formed the third eye to restore order, and fire emerged from his third eye to re-create light. The fierce light from his third eye is so powerful and destructive that henceforth he only opens it to destroy all that is unconscious, dark and dualistic in the universe. Shiva's third eye opens to end all illusion. The third eye, thus, is a symbol of wisdom, enlightenment and deep spiritual vision.

In India today, Hindus, especially women, who are devotees of Shiva wear a dot on their foreheads to show their devotion to Shiva. But culturally, the dot on the forehead of Indian women has become part of cosmetics. They do it to look beautiful. There is a funny story about that:

Finally, the Indian embassy in Ottawa has revealed the real meaning of the dot. It is like this. When a woman gets married in India, she brings a dowry into the union. On the night of the wedding, the groom scratches the dot on his bride's forehead to find out if he has won a convenience store, a gas station, a Dunkin Donut shop, or a motel in the United States. If the dot reveals none of the above, he must stay in India and answer telephone calls to offer technical support for US customers.

Jokes aside, I invite you to focus on the deeper meaning of the dot which is the third eye. It is the eye that helps us to look *beyond* what we see; it is the eye that enables us to see beyond the superficial. It focuses on the soul of the person standing in front of you, instead of the body. It helps you to see every ground as holy. The third eye helps you see miracles

everywhere, every day, in everything.

Apostle Paul talks about this eye when he tells the Ephesians: "I pray that the eyes of your heart may be enlightened in order that you may know the hope to which he has called you." (1:18)

Let me show you how you can always experience miracles, closer to home. All you have to do is open your third eye, and pay attention and look closely.

The human body is one of the most miraculous machines that God has ever created. We should meditate on every aspect of our body to see how beautifully and wonderfully we are made (Ps:139:14). Our body is with us all the time; we take it with us where ever we go. We don't pay much attention to it most of the time. We may pay attention to how it appears outside. But most people don't think about how it functions so perfectly to keep us healthy and alive.

I want you to meditate on just one aspect of our body: The digestive system.

Digestion begins in the mouth when the food is swallowed as a **boulus** down the esophagus to the stomach. At the junction of the esophagus and the stomach is a lid called the **epiglottis,** which closes when we swallow to protect the lungs from food passing into them. If that epiglottis does not open and close properly we will aspirate and die.

When it reaches the stomach the food is broken down into a semi-liquid mass called **chyme**. The chyme will not pass into the duodenum, the first foot of the small intestine, until the particles are one millimeter or less. Enzymes from the pancreas and bile from the liver enter the duodenum via the bile duct. The food now goes into the **jejunum** which is the next 9 feet of the small intestine and the absorption of fats, proteins and carbohydrates are done there. Vitamin B12 is absorbed in the **ileum** which is the last 12 feet of the small intestine.

The chyme then enters the large intestine or colon, about 4 or 5 feet long, which is called the ascending colon, transverse colon and the descending colon. The colon absorbs water, electrolytes and bile salts. The last five inches of the colon make up the rectum.

Did you know that our digestive system is about 25 feet long? If you stretch your esophagus, small intestine and large intestine, it will be 25 feet long, which is more than four times your height; but it is so nicely folded and tucked inside. It doesn't get mangled up or displaced whether you are sitting, standing, lying down, running or standing on your head.

In addition, now imagine a nine pound baby in the tummy of a pregnant woman. The entire digestive system and all the internal organs adjust in such a beautiful way to accommodate the needs and comfort of that baby too.

What I described is just a summary of the digestive process. Go to your computer and Google digestive system and you can read all the marvelous details of this process. For example, one of the unsolved puzzles of the digestive system is why the acid juice of the stomach, which is so toxic and powerful enough to dismantle and disintegrate the food, does not dissolve the tissue of the stomach itself?

For example, if you take that stomach acid and drink, you will die; but in the stomach it doesn't kill you.

Now, you can look at all these with your two eyes and dismiss it as a mere physiological process. Or you can look at it with your third eye and see it as a mystical dance initiated and choreographed by the great Sacred Mystery, we call God.

This God is the guardian of our epiglottis; He makes sure that the food doesn't go into our lungs. He makes sure that just the appropriate amount of enzymes and bile is processed each time we eat. He makes sure that the acids don't destroy our intestines.

As the chyme makes its way through the 25 feet of delicate plumbing, the simultaneous processes of absorption and elimination happens flawlessly. Remember that the liver, pancreas, heart, lungs and kidneys have to operate perfectly, too.

It is a mind boggling mystical dance only a divine choreographer can orchestrate so impeccably and perfectly. It is a miracle that happens within us all the time.

As Albert Einstein said, "you can live your life as if nothing is a miracle; or you can live your life as if everything is a miracle."

I invite you to choose the latter and walk into the mystery of God each day, with your physical eyes closed and the third eye wide open.

21. Significance of Insignificance
Text: Mark 12: 41-44

Jesus sat down opposite the place where the offerings were put and watched the crowd putting their money into the temple treasury. Many rich people threw in large amounts. But a poor widow came and put in two very small copper coins, worth only a fraction of a penny.

Calling his disciples to him, Jesus said, "I tell you the truth, this poor widow has put more into the treasury than all the others. They all gave out of their wealth; but she, out her poverty, put in everything—all she had to live on."

Recently I paid for a three year subscription to *Time* magazine. Last week I got a postcard in the mail which said: "You have overpaid by one penny. We can extend the subscription for one week or we could send you a check for the penny. Please call customer service at…"

I have never seen anything like this; a huge corporation like Time Inc. concerned about returning a penny to me. I did not call them, because that phone call would cost me more than a penny. If they mail the check, the postage will be 45 cents. It took 28 cents to mail me the post card informing me that I had overpaid by one penny! Only in America! I wish all the corporations were like Time, Inc.

The penny that you are holding in your hand is the lowest, least valuable and easily expendable coin in the American financial system. That is why it is easily tossed around and stumped upon. You can buy nothing with a penny. It is so worthless that many people don't even bother to pick it up if they see a penny on the ground. On the other hand, if you find a nickel or a dime or quarter you are more likely to pick it up. That is why you don't see nickels, dimes and quarters lying on the street. But the penny that no one cares about is found everywhere, ignored, neglected and abandoned.

I want to show you today, how useful and powerful the penny actually is in the big financial picture. Let us say, we eliminate the penny and use the nickel as the lowest coin. That will increase our taxes by about two billion dollars a year. Because the 6% sales tax will have to be increased to 11% and if they ever want to increase it again, they have to do 16%...see where it is going?

It will also affect the gas prices by another 6 billion. Let us say, price per gallon at the pump this morning is $3.55; by this evening it could go up to $3.60 and tomorrow to $3.65. Without the little penny as a buffer, prices will go up exponentially.

Another problem is that retailers will not be able to advertise their price as $9.99 or $19.99 or $29.99 which is by the way, the biggest marketing ploy of the century. It is so deceptive and we unconsciously think that we are paying 9 or 19 dollars, but in fact we are paying 10 or 20. Another problem with not having the penny around is that Herman Cain will never be able to say 9-9-9.

So, the penny is much more valuable and useful than we think, and that is why the treasury keeps minting them even though it costs 1.5 cents to produce 1 cent, because zinc is expensive.

I want to show you this morning, how this penny can be used as a tool for prayer and spiritual growth. If I see a penny on the ground, I always pick it up. I will never ignore it as insignificant and worthless. There should be a sign on my back that says: "This Man Stops for Every Penny," like the sign behind some trucks: "This Vehicle Stops at All Rail Crossings."

I always pick up several pennies during my morning walk which I make through the parking lot of a middle school. You know kids drop money everywhere because they are careless; besides, they won't bother to pick up a penny because they don't know the value of money.

Last year, I tried an experiment to see how much money I will have if I were to add up all the pennies I had picked up during the year. I put them in a separate jar and by the end of the year, I had collected $28.94. That would buy me one decent dinner, 6 happy meals, or 7 gallons of gas or 8 gallons of milk or 28 lottery tickets.

You get the idea, it can be worthwhile.

But more than the economic value, the little penny for me, is a spiritual tool. There are some profound spiritual truths inscribed on that small piece of zinc. I don't know if you have paid attention to it; that is why I gave you a penny this morning.

Feel it in your hand. Take a look and pay attention to the words on it. There are 8 different inscriptions on it: *One Cent, The year it was minted, Lincoln Memorial, Face of Lincoln, Liberty, United States of America, E Pluribus Unum,* and *In God we trust.*

The penny contains the essence and the soul of this nation.

So this is what I do when I pick up a penny. First I say, "Thank you Lord for the abundance." The penny doesn't look like abundance, but it is the symbol all the abundance in my life, food shelter, clothing, transportation, etc. I thank God that I have enough money to meet all my obligations.

Then I look at the face of Lincoln and that reminds me to pray for our president. Regardless of our party affiliations, we should pray for our president, because he is the leader of our nation. It is the most difficult job in the world and he needs our prayers.

Then there is the word *Liberty*. You can spend a whole 15 minutes thanking God for the freedoms we enjoy in this country. The reason why people from every corner of the globe want to come to the United States is because of the freedoms we have. We can sit in this church and worship without being harassed by anyone. Many people in the world don't have that freedom. So, I thank God for the freedom of worship, among many other freedoms that I enjoy.

E Pluribus Unum--that phrase always brings me chills. *From many, one*. That is a profound statement of what America is all about; people from all over the world, coming together to form one union. The United States is the only nation on earth which has people from all other nations. There is no other country like this. If you go to India, it is full of just Indians born and raised there. Nobody immigrates to India. I hold that penny in my hand I pray for continued unity and peace in this nation. As a Christian, it is also an opportunity to think of all peoples as members of the one body of Christ.

Then I look at the year in which the penny was born. Look at the year on your penny. Mine was minted in 1992. It is 19 years old. During those 19 years, it must have traveled to thousands of places. May be it stayed in somebody's house, ignored for many years. May it stayed out in the cold under a bridge for some years. It must have passed through the hands of millions of people.

The penny you are holding in your hand is a silent witness to the sadness and gladness, the triumphs and failures or the loneliness and celebration of thousands of people. The energy of every person who touched this penny over the years is part of it, and now, I get to share my energy with all those people. I see myself connected to all those people. I say a prayer for them and there I feel a sense of love, unity and connection.

Then there are those four powerful words on the penny. *In God*

We Trust. I surrender my life to God in the morning, always knowing that regardless of what happens this day, God is going to take care of me.

See how deep and powerful, meaningful and valuable, an insignificant penny can be? Jesus knew the importance and value of apparently insignificant things and that is why he pays special attention to the widow and her penny. According to the story, it was not even a whole penny; they were two small copper coins, worth only a fraction of a penny! And still Jesus pays attention to that.

Many wealthy people were putting sizable amounts of money into the box, but Jesus is not impressed. Jesus was touched by the two small copper coins of a poor widow. He called his disciples and told them: "This widow has contributed more than all the others. They gave from their surplus, she gave all she had."

Yes, Jesus takes note of everything we do, the mundane and the minutia, the smallest and simplest of our behaviors and gestures. He is not watching us as a "big brother" but to let us know that, everything, which means those things that we consider so insignificant, is significant in the eyes of God.

It doesn't matter how much we give, what matters is HOW we give. When we give all that we have, with love and generosity it is pleasing to God, and it makes a big difference.

Mother Teresa is someone who understood the deep meaning of the widow's mite. She had no worldly power, she was not a king or president and she had no military at her disposal. She never donated millions to any cause. All she did was patch up the wounds of the poorest of the poor in the dirty slums of Calcutta. But the impact of this one humble, diminutive woman, who did the simple act of caring for the least among us, is enormous.

It is Mother Theresa who said, that **all of us may not be able to do great things; but all of us can do small things with great love.**

I wanted to bring you this message today, because, yesterday was *Make a Difference Day* in America. For the last 18 years, *USA Weekend Magazine* has designated the 4th Saturday of October as *Make a Difference Day*. The thinking behind the celebration is that all of us, regardless of how insignificant we consider ourselves to be, can make a difference in the world. Yesterday, 3 million people participated in the act of making a little difference in the life of their community.

You might say things like, "what can I do to make any difference in this huge world of 7 billion people, I am just one person, nobody knows me, I don't have any power." I used to think like that until I started working as a hospice chaplain. A few years ago, I had an experience that changed my views on this subject.

I had this 92 year old patient named Angela whom I used to visit every Friday. She had no family or friends. The hospice team was her family. She used to eagerly wait for my visit. One Friday, I found her to be very upset and distressed. Her TV had stopped working. For the elderly, TV is their only companion. Some people just keep it on, to mask the deadly silence of loneliness.

Angela was on a limited budget and she didn't have the money to pay a repairman. She asked me if I could repair her TV. Being totally mechanically challenged, I didn't dare. When Angela went to the kitchen to make coffee, I just looked around the TV and to my surprise, found that the TV was not plugged into the outlet. I plugged it in, and *Judge Judy* came on. "Angela, it is a miracle," I cried out in excitement. She couldn't believe her eyes. She hugged and kissed me, and thanked me profusely.

"You made my day; thank you, thank you; you have no idea what this means to me; I thank God for sending you here."

That day, I realized that a simple act as plugging in a TV can make a huge difference in somebody's life. I also decided that day, never to judge the impact of my behavior on others based on my perceptions, because, what I consider to be insignificant, could be very significant for somebody else.

Through the story of the widow's mite, Jesus reminds us that everything we do is important in the eyes of God, so that we may do it with compassion and devotion; that we won't look at anything casually, or treat anyone callously; that we will pay attention to small things, embrace the moment and cherish each person that is before us.

22. Re-thinking Heaven
Text: Luke 17:20-22

Once having been asked by the Pharisees when the Kingdom of God would come, Jesus replied, "The Kingdom of God does not come with your careful observation, nor will people say, "here it is or there it is, because the Kingdom of God is within you!"

An 85 year old couple, married for 60 years, died in a car crash. They were in good health the last ten years mainly due to her interest in health food, and exercise.

When they reached the pearly gates, St. Peter took them to their mansion which was decked out with a beautiful kitchen, a master bath and Jacuzzi.

As they "oohed and aahed" the old man asked Peter how much all this was going to cost.

"It's free," Peter replied, "this is Heaven."
Next they went out back to survey the championship golf course. They would have golfing privileges every day.

The old man asked, "What are the green fees?"

Peter's reply, "This is heaven, you play for free." Next they went to the club house and saw the lavish buffet lunch with the cuisines of the world laid out.

"How much to eat?" asked the old man.

"Don't you understand yet? This is heaven, it is free!"
"Well, where are the low fat and low cholesterol tables?" the old

man asked timidly. Peter said: "That's the best part...you can eat as much as you like of whatever you like and you never get fat and you never get sick. This is heaven."

With that the old man went into a hissy fit, throwing down his hat and stomping on it, and shrieking wildly.

Peter and the man's wife trying to calm him down, asked him what was wrong. The old man looked at his wife and said:

"This is all your fault. If it weren't for your blasted bran muffin and healthy diet, I could have been here ten years ago!"

When we hear the word "heaven," there is an image that pops up in our mind. It is usually an image of a place where there is joy and happiness and eternal rest 24 hours a day, 7 days a week. It is always imagined as *a place* above the clouds...a place with pearly gates and singing angels--a place where St. Peter stands at the gate and admits people based on how they lived their lives. The good ones enter heaven and the bad ones go down to hell. The idea of heaven and hell as locations is so entrenched in our consciousness that it is so hard to change it.
.
These images of heaven and hell are centuries old. People who lived 3000 years ago, who did not have access to any of the modern understandings of geography and astronomy came up with these images. Should we just believe them or should we ask questions about it?

May be a different understanding of heaven could help live our lives on earth a little better.

That is where my sermon title comes in. It is taken from the cover of *Time* magazine dated, April 16, 2012. The author has some new perspectives on heaven and how they can help us live better.
I like to share with you, my personal beliefs about heaven. You

don't have to buy into it. But I like you to think about it.

First of all, let me say this very clearly. **Yes, I believe in heaven and hell, but I don't believe heaven is a gated community with pearly gates located up there or hell is fiery furnace down under.**

Then you might say, but Jesus said in John 14 that "there are many mansions in my father's house, I am going to prepare a place for you." But Jesus also said: "Don't say the Kingdom is here or there, because the Kingdom of God is within you." Jesus said, "I am the vine you are the branches." That doesn't mean Jesus is a tree and we are branches with leaves. Jesus said: "I am the bread from heaven." That doesn't mean he is a loaf of bread either.

Jesus was speaking in symbols and images. He was trying to express the inexpressible using words.

We have to be very careful when we say, *" It is in the bible and the case is closed."*

The idea of a heaven "up" there and hell "down" below is based on the notion of a flat earth. When the Bible was written centuries ago, the bible writers thought that the earth was flat. We cannot blame them for thinking that, because they did not have telescopes then. There were no scientific discoveries. The primitive people of biblical times looked around and they saw the earth as flat. They looked up and they saw sky and they thought it was the dome covering the earth. They believed in a 'hamburger universe:' Heaven up there, earth in the middle, and hell down.

But now we know better. Since the time of Copernicus and Galileo, we know that the earth is indeed round. In a round concept, there is no up or down.
Bishop NT Wright, a prominent Anglican bishop has a book titled

Surprised by Hope. It is a modern day discussion of heaven. He writes: **Heaven is not the longed for destination of dying people; but the realm of God that intersects our universe in such a way, as to transform the way we live.**

Pay attention to the two words he uses: "Intersects and transforms." Heaven is at the intersection where God and we meet. Where is that intersection? Is it far away, up there, where we go only after we die?

The notion that we have to live this life being miserable and unhappy until we die, is such a bad deal.

Jesus did not come into this world to take us to heaven after we die; He came into this world to help us experience heaven during this life.

That is why the first words out of his mouth when he started his public ministry were:

The Kingdom of heaven is AT HAND. He did not say, the Kingdom of heaven is in a faraway place that you will get to go at a later time. It is now. That is why in the only prayer Jesus taught, he said: "Our father...thy Kingdom come on EARTH as it is in heaven."

Heaven is not a future reward for a good life, but a present experience of life as good.

So don't ask, "how to go to heaven?" which implies traveling somewhere else; don't ask, "Are you in heaven," which implies you have to **enter** into something that is outside of you. **The right question is: "Is heaven in you?"**

It is a dimension within you that is calm and peaceful, serene and joyful, a dimension that permeates your entire being, something that you experience where ever you are, and take it with you where ever you go. You will not wait for it; you will not look for it somewhere else, but you will feel it inside; that is why Jesus said: "The Kingdom of God is within you." If you don't feel that inside now, you are unlikely to feel it later, anywhere else or with anybody else.

Heaven is the intersection where God and we meet. Because God is everywhere, that intersection is everywhere.

Royal Palm Christian Church is such an intersection. We feel it when we come here. Walking around during worship, and giving and receiving hugs from each other is heaven; for me walking down Atlantic Blvd and watching the beautiful sunset is heaven.

Some of you know that Johnny, my autistic son, had a summer job at the Marriott Hotel in Parkland. Seeing his first paycheck, with his name on it with all the withholdings and deductions and the net pay at the bottom and knowing that he can do some work, that was heaven for me.

Watching our dog Sally snuggling up to Judy on the sofa and sleeping in her lap totally loved and comfortable, now, that is a slice of heaven.

The other day I was eating a mango. It was sweet and juicy. Then I started thinking: The tree that produced this fabulous fruit is planted in dirt; the fertilizers it absorbed are toxic and poisonous. The tiny mango that appeared on the branches, three months ago, was bitter and pungent. Then it transformed and became this delicious juicy fruit. Eating that and thinking about the marvelous and mysterious beauty of God's creation, that was heaven.

But how can we consider these ordinary, mundane activities like eating a mango or watching a dog sleep be compared to heaven? Consider, what Jesus said: "The Kingdom of Heaven is like a woman kneading flower in her kitchen;" "the Kingdom of Heaven is like a merchant looking for pearls;" "the Kingdom of Heaven is like ten virgins who took their lamps to meet the bridegroom;" "the Kingdom of Heaven is like a farmer sowing seeds in his field."

All earthly activities…performed by ordinary people…on the earth...during this life!

What I am saying is that we have to try to make every experience in life a heavenly one. Even the painful and hardest experiences have the seed of heaven hidden within them, like a mango seed growing in dirt, producing a juicy fruit. All we have to do is to open our eyes and start seeing it with the eye of the soul.

Remember these words of Neale Donald Walsch: **Heaven is not a place to go to, but realizing that you are already ther**

23. From Stressed to Blessed
Text: Mark 4: 35-41

That day when evening came, he said to his disciples, "Let us go over to the other side." Leaving the crowd behind, they took him along, just as he was, in the boat. There were also other boats with him. A furious squall came up, and the waves broke over the boat, so that it was nearly swamped. Jesus was in the stern, sleeping on a cushion. The disciples woke him and said to him, "Teacher, don't you care if we drown?"

He got up, rebuked the wind and said to the waves, "Quiet! Be still!" then the wind died down and it was completely calm. He said to his disciples, "Why are you so afraid? Do you still have no faith?" They were terrified and asked each other, "Who is this, even the wind and the waves obey him!"

These days, everybody is stressed out. There are good reasons for it, both personal and national. Personally, people may be suffering from health problems, money problems, relationship problems, and a whole lot of other problems.

And nationally, there are plenty of things to get stressed out: unemployment, recession and terrorism to name a few.

I Googled the word 'stress' and there are 159 million entries on it in the internet. There are hundreds of books and thousands of articles explaining what stress is and a thousand remedies to deal with it.

According to a recent survey, 85 percent of the American workforce experience high stress on the job. The world is more competitive and less predictable than before. Christians are not immune to stress.

Work is not the only source of stress. Relationships, managing a home or budget, parenting, and crises are few of the things that can lead to a feeling of being stressed out.

I have a file on stress and I found some materials in it. One talks about "Stress: the invisible enemy." And there is a checklist of symptoms of stress. Some of the emotional symptoms are: irritability, angry outbursts, depression, restlessness, anxiety, tendency to cry, and tendency to blame. Some of the physical symptoms are: headaches, knots in stomach, tight muscles, grinding teeth, rapid breathing, clammy hands, nausea, shaky feeling and skin rash.

Since stress is such a huge problem in society, we have come up with remedies. There are thousands of stress management seminars conducted all over the country every day. Many people engage in stress reducing exercises. In spite of all that, people are still stressed out.

I was at a stress management seminar last week, offered to us at work. This lady, who is a mental health expert, gave us a two hour presentation with colorful slides, explaining stress, causes of stress and remedies for stress. She gave us a list of things we could do to reduce stress. There were 63 bullet point items on the list.

One of them was to take a vacation to reduce stress. So you are stressed out, and you take a nice cruise. You feel great while you are cruising, visiting beautiful places, buying nice souvenirs, and eating great food and over eating deserts at the midnight buffet. But when you return home after such a great cruise, you are stressed out again, because you have to deal with the same stressful environment you left behind before you went on the cruise, not to mention the added stress of paying off the credit card bill that you incurred while cruising, and worrying about the extra pounds you gained. Nothing has really changed, except for a week of respite.

For me, this is the wrong way to deal with stress, because, it is an unending cycle. Stress, cruise and more stress.

Let me show you another paper, listing 70 stress busters. Some of the items on this list are: Take a breath, give hugs, exercise, sing a song, eat right, call a friend, ask for help, smile, avoid clutter, use proper lighting, have a hobby, talks things out, learn to relax, reward yourself, be flexible, say no, be faithful, read good books, etc.

I have a huge problem with this list, because it does not address the root problem of stress. All these are short term solutions. Doing these things is like treating the symptoms, not the cause.

If you study the list carefully, you will see that each one of those 70 items listed is a BEHAVIOR. None of them is a BELIEF. If you don't have sound beliefs to support your behaviors, the behaviors won't last. Behaviors without beliefs are like a body without a brain, a car without an engine, or like a kite without a string.

In other words, this list is all about DOING, and not about BEING. Trying to DO things without thinking about BEING, is a prescription for failure.

So I am going to teach you today, as to how to live a stress free life. If you follow what I am going to tell you, you will be able to reduce 90 percent of your stress. It is about Jesus. It is not about believing in Jesus, because I know a lot of stressed-out believers. It is about understanding Jesus and following his example.

When you look at the Jesus of the gospels, you never see him being stressed out. You see him to be calm, peaceful and easy going. But life was not easy for Jesus. As a matter of fact, Jesus lived in a very stressful environment. People misunderstood him, his family disowned him, his disciples betrayed and denied him, and the authorities wanted to trap him or kill him. Now, if that is not a stressful situation, I don't know what is. In the midst of all these highly stress-inducing situations, we see a peaceful Jesus. How did he do that?

Before I answer that, I want you to have a clear understanding of what stress is. I have to say that all the definitions of stress in books and articles are incorrect. Every one of them defines stress as an EXTERNAL event. **When you read those books or attend those stress management seminars, you get the impression that stress is something that is OUT THERE. That is the wrong approach.**

When was the last time you went to the supermarket and bought a pound of stress? **What shelf in which aisle of Publix displays stress as an item with a price tag on it?** Is there ever a 'sale' on it, like buy one get one free?

I am sure you have felt stressed out while you were inside the store, stressed out because you could not find the item you were looking for, or the item was more expensive than you thought, or you were standing in an express line for ten items or less and you are counting how many items the person in front has and fuming inside. Or you are stressed out because the clerk told you that your coupons had expired.

Yes, you can feel stressed out in a supermarket, but you cannot purchase it there.

What I am trying to say to you is that stress is an INTERNAL reality. It is not out there, it is in your mind. It is an INTERPRETATION of an external event. It is a belief about an event. So, if you can change your interpretation, or your belief, you can remove the stress.

For example, let us say, I go to Disney World with my son. And we both ride the roller coaster. At the end of the ride, I am angry, shaking and stressed out but my son, Tommy, is happy, laughing and totally exhilarated: same external experience, two different interpretations.

Or, look at a train: Too many people in a particular car will be described as 'crowded,' but too many people in a night club will be described as 'atmosphere.' Same reality; two different interpretations.

So, there is no actual stress or anxiety in the world; it is your thoughts that create those false beliefs. As I said, **you cannot package stress, buy it, sell it, touch it or see it. There are only people engaged in stressful thinking**. That is why Webster's Dictionary defines stress as "**mental tension.**" It is a mental reality, and if you can train your mind to interpret reality differently, the stress will just disappear.

When we think stressfully, we create reactions in the body. They reveal themselves as nausea, high blood pressure, indigestion, ulcers, headaches, increased heart rate and a zillion other feelings, from minor discomfort to major life threatening illness.

Let me give you an example. I am standing in line at the drugstore to drop off a prescription. And the person ahead of me is talking to the pharmacist asking him a series of seemingly inane questions and my stress producing ego gets annoyed. I am standing there fuming. My inner dialogue might go like this: *I am being victimized; there is always someone ahead of me fumbling with money or coupons, or can't find the insurance card, and has to ask silly questions to keep me waiting in this line. Where do these people come from? Can't they get organized before they get on line?*

Instead of these thoughts, if I were to say to myself, *Paul stop taking yourself so seriously; life is too short to get upset over silly things like this; if f I die today, will this matter?* Immediately, I make the shift from stressed to blessed.

So don't blame stress as something out there; always pay attention to what you are saying about the event to yourself. Monitor the dialogue going on in your brain, pay attention to your thoughts. And when you change your thoughts from negative to positive, you change your life from being stressful ordeal in the vale of tears to a blissful journey in the kindom of heaven.

Let us see what is happening to the disciples in today's text. They were out on a boat in the Sea of Galilee. We are not talking about the *Oasis of the Seas,* the 5,000 passenger capacity cruise ship owned by Carnival Cruise Lines. It was most probably a wooden boat. And the story says that there was a squall and the boat was nearly swamped.

And the disciples were frightened. As they began to panic, they woke up Jesus, asking him: "Don't you care, we are drowning? When they did this there was a dialogue going on in their heads. It might have been something like this: "Oh my God, the storm is coming, the boat is going to capsize and we are all going to die." Their reaction shows that is how they interpreted the external event of the storm.

On the other hand, if they were to say to themselves: "We are seasoned fishermen, we have seen this before; if the boat sinks we can swim; may be the storm will subside; If not, we have the Master with us, who has walked on water, who has healed the sick and raised the dead. As long as we are with him, we are going to be okay." Apparently, that is not what they were thinking!

What does Jesus do? He is sleeping through the storm. All the commotion happening outside is not affecting him. He has no fearful thoughts; and he has no alarming reactions; He wakes up and says: "Be quiet; be still." And the storm subsides; everything is peaceful.

For Jesus, the calm in the middle of storm came from inside; that peace in the midst of chaos came from his closeness to his Father. The storm does not control Jesus, but Jesus controls the storm.

Jesus who calmed the storm in the Sea of Galilee is with us. The question is: "Is Jesus asleep in our lives?"

The world is the sea and we are the boats; if Jesus is asleep in us, we will be tossed around like a cork in the ocean of life and that is exactly what is happening to a lot of people. We need to keep Jesus awake in us; if we can think, feel and act like Jesus, the so called stressful events that happen around us, will never control our lives. We will be transformed from being stressed to blessed.

24. We Belong to Each Other
Text: John 20: 19-23

On the evening of the first day of the week, when the disciples were together, with the doors locked for fear of the Jews, Jesus came and stood among them and said, "Peace be with you!" After he said this, he showed them his hands and side. The disciples were overjoyed when they saw the Lord.

Again, Jesus said, "Peace be with you! As the Father has sent me, I am sending you." And with that he breathed on them and said, "Receive the Holy Spirit. If you forgive anyone his sins, they are forgiven; if you do not forgive them, they are not forgiven."

Today is *World Sunday for Peace,* celebrated by Christian Churches around the world. Pastor Craig is in Jamaica this week, attending the First International Ecumenical Peace Convocation, organized by the World Council of Churches. Thousands of delegates from around the world will gather and talk about ways and means to bring about peace in the world. It is a good thing because, as a UN secretary General once said, *Thinking about peace is already a powerful means to contribute to peace.*

We also know that this conference is not going to bring about world peace, because we have been celebrating *World Peace Day* since it was established by the United Nations in 1981. The Catholic Church has celebrated *Peace Sunday* for many years. Numerous attempts have been made to bring about peace in the Middle East. The Middle East envoy, Senator George Mitchell just resigned last week. In spite of all our efforts, peace seems to be a mirage.

I am reminded of a story of a journalist assigned to the Jerusalem bureau of CNN. She had an apartment overlooking the Wailing Wall. Daily, she watched an old man vigorously praying in front of the wall. One day she asked him: "Every day I see you praying at the wall; how long have you done this and what are you praying for?"

"I have come here daily for 25 years. I pray for peace between Arabs and Jews. I pray that all hatred in the world end, and I pray for all children of God to live in peace and harmony."

"How does it make you feel that after all these years of praying, your prayers are not answered?"

The old man looked at her sadly and said: *It is like talking to a wall.*

World Peace seems like such an impossible dream. We have lack of peace in our country too. We may not be wounding people with weapons; but words can be more deadly than weapons. Just watch cable TV and you will find out. Now that election season is heating up, you will see more division and disunity in the country. How about your souls? Do you feel peace inside?

I invite you to approach peacemaking with a whole new attitude, because traditional methods of achieving peace have failed. You know why? Because our primary focus was to create peace out there, in the community, in the nation, in the Middle East, in the world. It has not worked so far and it will not work, because we are operating from a basic fallacy, and that is, peace is something that is out there.

The greatest threat to world peace is not nuclear weapons, but nuclear hearts filled with hatred, jealousy and anger. In other words, the greatest threat to world peace is not warheads, but war heads.

And how do we develop such nuclear hearts? It is developed in our mental laboratory using a pervasive substance called ignorance, and the product that is created is called SEPARATION ILLUSION.

What is *Separation Illusion*? It is the belief that we are separate from each other. The thinking that as nations, religions and races, we are separate from other nations, religions and races, and that we are better than others; that our religion is better than their religion, and that our interests should be taken care of regardless of what happens to others.

I call this an illusion because if you really think about it, you will find that we are not separate, but intimately connected to each other. It will take some deep reflection to find that connection. It is not readily visible to our external eyes and superficial minds.

Let me give you an example. Last year, I had knee surgery for a torn meniscus. About six people were directly involved in my surgery, but about six billion were indirectly involved to make it all happen that day.

What do I mean by that? Early in the morning, I took a shower in the water that was supplied by the city of Coral Springs. I was thinking of the thousands of people who were involved in the harnessing, production, purification and channeling of that water supply to my house at my home address: the people who manufactured the pipes that made that water flow safe; the companies that made the water purification chemicals; the people who made the hot water tank in my house; the technicians who installed it. When I think like that, the number of people involved in giving me a hot shower that morning, multiplies by thousands.

Remember, the day has barely started, and millions are still going to be involved.

I was wearing a shirt that morning with a label that read: *Made in Bangladesh; 100% cotton*. Usually people don't pay attention to these things, but I do, and it has a lot to do with the peace and joy I feel in my life.

I thought of the thousands of people who were involved in making that shirt, starting with the poor villagers who produced the cotton, a grandmother who might have woven that cotton into threads in a small factory in a remote village. Her emotions of fear and hope or hopelessness have been woven into the threads that made that shirt which is now covering my body. I think of the people who made the machine that stitched my shirt together; the person, who folded it, packed it, sealed and placed it on a truck to be exported to the United Sates. The fears, cares and energies of all those people are part of the fabric I am wearing that day.

Then I think of the train that transported it to the nearest airport in Bangladesh, and off to a cargo plane bound for Arkansas, the headquarters of *Wal-Mart*. From there it is unloaded, coded and re-routed into a truck that goes a 1000 miles to a *Wal-Ma*rt in Coral Springs. Think of the thousands of employees whose joint effort made that shirt appear on a rack, and I pick it up, pay for it with a credit card, issued by a bank that has another ten thousand employees, who make sure that *Wal-Mart* is paid on my behalf. And the $19.99 I paid for that shirt becomes part of the wages of an unknown employee at *Wal-Mart* who in turn buys food for her family with that money and she is connected to how many people, I can only imagine. You see the endless connections with people that make it all possible.

The day has barely begun, and I have not gotten to the Surgery Center yet. My wife drives me there in a car that has 2200 different parts. Those 2200 parts of the car have been touched by the energy, imagination, and efforts of another million people, not here, but somewhere in Japan.

Then I walk into the Surgery Center, and there is the girl at the front desk, who registers me on a Dell Computer which has 5000 parts, that was made in China…and now a billion Chinese people are getting involved in my life that day.

Then I am taken into the prep room, and I am surrounded by half a dozen people, nurses, anesthesiologist, the surgeon, and recovery room personnel. I am thinking of all the people who are connected to them by extension, their families, friends, the communities they belong to etc.

Then they put me under, using this sedation medication that was manufactured in a medical lab in Nebraska, shipped via Fed Ex planes and a Fed Ex driver brings it to the facility. An unknown Fed Ex driver and all the people in his life have now gotten involved in my life.
And then there is this million dollar medical equipment with a zillion parts, lights, camera and laser beams that will make three holes on my knee, will probe the damaged

area, and this doctor whom I have seen only twice in my entire life, will scrape it, repair it and make it right.

That morning, I was held tenderly and directly in the hands of six human beings, but I was indirectly supported and lovingly sustained by the energy of six billion people. That is how I experience God: through my connectedness to people who are created in the image and likeness of God.

And the funny thing is that I was completely unconscious, lying down helplessly, totally at the mercy of a group of strangers. But the reality is that they are not strangers; they are strangers only in a superficial sense. In a deeper sense, on the level of the soul, they are my brothers and sisters, sharing my same humanity.

This is just one scenario of a single human interaction. This happens in all of our lives, every day. You don't have to go into surgery to experience it. Where ever there is a human interaction or transaction, this scenario of connectedness and interdependence plays out all the time.

And that is my greatest argument for peace. If we are connected to people, we cannot be at war with them.

We don't have peace in the world because we think we are strangers to each other; that the other person or the other nation has nothing to do with us; that we are in competition with each other; that other people are our enemies; that other religions are inferior to ours; that enemies need to be destroyed.

That kind of separatist thinking will never bring peace in the world. That is why Mother Teresa who won the Nobel Prize for Peace in 1979 said it so powerfully: ***If we have no*** *peace, it is because we have forgotten that we belong to each other.*

So, the way of peace is primarily, an inner process, a changing of our consciousness about the unity of humanity. Today, I invite to raise your consciousness to a higher level: **From the lowest level, which is the level of division, disunity, and exclusion, to the highest level of inclusion, unity and wholeness.**

This is the message Apostle Paul gives in Eph. 2. Paul is talking about the unity between the Gentiles and the Jews who considered themselves separate from each other. He says that *Christ is our peace destroying the barrier, the dividing wall of hostility between them. He came and preached peace to you who were far away and peace to those who were near. Consequently, you are no longer foreigners and aliens, but fellow citizens with God's people and members of God's household, built on the foundations of the apostles and prophets, with Christ himself as the chief cornerstone.*

I love that phrase, **members of God's household.** How can we fight with another human being or another group if we are all members of God's household.
Jesus' prescription for peace is also unity. That is why his last prayer on earth was for unity among his disciples and all peoples. The first thing Jesus said to his disciples after resurrection was PEACE. Peace be with you. In today's reading, we see it both as a greeting and a mission. Jesus wants us to experience peace and be peacemakers.

I like to end with a prayer my friend Piero repeats every month in Coral Springs, after the Silent Peace Walk on first Saturdays of the month.

Peace in our hearts brings peace to our families.
Peace in our families brings peace to our communities.
Peace in our communities brings peace to our nations.
Peace in our nations brings peace to the world.
Let there be peace on earth, and let it begin with me.

25. Is it True, Is it Necessary and Is it Kind?
Text: Romans 1:28-32

Furthermore, since they did not think it worthwhile to retain the knowledge of God, he gave them over to depraved mind, to do what ought not to be done. They have become filled with every kind of wickedness, evil, greed and depravity. They are full of envy, murder, strife, deceit and malice; they are gossips, slanderers, God-haters, insolent, arrogant and boastful; they invent ways of doing evil; they disobey their parents; they are senseless, faithless, heartless, and ruthless. Although they know God's righteous decree that those who do such things deserve death, they not only continue to do these very things but also approve of those who practice them.

We live in an "information age." Today, any information you need about anybody or anything is literally at your finger tips and is available within seconds.

You remember the days when salesmen used to go from door to door, selling *Encyclopedia Britannica*? They used to come to your house to make a presentation and sell those humongous volumes to you for a hefty price. Lot of families with young children bought them. Fifteen years ago, we almost bought a set. There is no one selling or buying encyclopedias anymore. If you want to do research on any topic, it is just a click away.

So the internet is a good thing for collecting data and information. But it can also be a curse. That curse comes in the form of misinformation, half truths, distortions of truth and outright lies. A lot of it comes from the blogosphere. A blog is basically an on line diary containing your thoughts, feelings, views, ideas and opinions. In olden times, people use to write them in a journal with pen or pencils. Today they write them using a computer and publish them on the internet. I have a blog too.

A blog that is used properly can be beneficial to the writer and the public. But in the hands of evil people, it can be very dangerous. It can distort truth, destroy careers, and destruct lives. One recent story that comes to mind is the story of Shirley Sherrod, an employee at the USDA in Atlanta.

Shirley Sherrod is an African American. A few years ago, she gave a speech to the NAACP. During that speech, she said that she struggled in her heart about giving approval for a white farmer 20 years ago. She thought of revenge first, because white people had hurt black people. But she overcame that feeling and did the right thing.

A conservative blogger named Andrew Briebart edited her 20 minute speech in such a way that she was portrayed as a racist on his blog. She was instantly fired from her job at the USDA. Later they found out that the blogger had distorted the truth and she was offered the job back. But she did not take it.

Another curse of the information age is the 24/7 cable channels, with self-proclaimed pundits on each one of them, mostly spewing venom on the airwaves. Remember the days when we had just three major networks, and we got the news from them at 6.30 PM on weekdays? We don't have to wait for the evening news any more.

Most of the stuff that comes out of cable channels these days is not news. They are opinions of pundits with an agenda, and they make statements that are so outrageous and untrue. One example that comes to mind is the phrase "death panels" which was used during the health care debate in 2010. Those two words: "death panels" were typed on a twitter message from Sarah Palin, and it went viral and created so much confusion, and a lot of people believed it.

I can tell you for a fact NOWHERE in the health care bill the phrase "death panels" appears. What is suggested is that in the case of terminally ill patients, where extensive and expensive treatments won't do any good, the doctor should discuss the option of hospice with patients and families. They twisted the idea about a hospice consultation like a pretzel and made it into death panels, and frightened people and an unsuspecting and fickle populace believed it.

Another tragic casualty of the information age is a teenager named Megan Meir. On October 16, 2006, Megan Meir of Missouri, who was 13 years old, committed suicide by hanging in her closet.

Megan had a neighbor by the name of Lori Drew who was 43 years old. She had a daughter who was Megan's age. This mother and daughter took part in an online hoax, using a *MySpace* account. They created a fake boy named "Josh Evans" who befriended and flirted with Megan online. The boy did not exist. It was a lie. Shortly before Megan's death, the comments from Josh and some other Internet users turned cruel, with "Josh" sending a message to Megan saying: *The world would be better without Megan Meir.* The young girl could not handle that message; she killed herself the next day.

The bottom line is that the so called information age has

become largely, an age of misinformation.

The internet, and blogs and the social media like *Facebook* and *Twitter*, can be good if used responsibly; but they can create havoc in the hands of malicious people and a lot of it is happening these days.

What is a disciple to do? None of us will act in the extreme ways I have described. But all of us can, unconsciously be part of a culture that causes disharmony and distress by the way we talk or react to the incessant chatter that is out there.

Today's scripture passage lists the sins of a reprobate, debased and depraved mind. In this awful list, fornication, wickedness, murder, gossip and slander are included. Our conscience might tell us that gossiping and slandering are wrong, but we may not realize the awfulness of these sins. You know why? Because they are so common. Unlike fornication and murder which are committed by only a minority, gossip and slander are almost universal. Because of this, they have become "acceptable" sins, even in Christian circles.

Gossip is idle talk, usually negative, spoken about someone who is not a part of the conversation. Much of what a gossiper says may be mere rumor, hearsay or sensationalized. Because the gossiper knows that gossip is wrong, he usually begins by saying "I hate to say this but I am so concerned about…." or "Since you mentioned it…." or "between you and me and the wall…"

Gossipers flatter us when they choose to share 'confidential information' with us, but beware of the fact that more often, those who gossip **to us** will also gossip **about us.**

Gossip and slander are grievous sins, and that is why Apostle Paul tells Ephesians: *Do not let any unwholesome talk come out of your mouths, but only what is helpful for building others up according to their needs, that it may benefit those who listen. And do not grieve the Holy Spirit… Holy Spirit with whom you were sealed for the day of redemption.* Talking ill of people and spreading misinformation is the same as grieving the Holy Spirit.

Paul continues: *Get rid of all bitterness, all passion, and anger, hard words, slander, and malice of every kind. Be kind to one another, compassionate, and mutually forgiving just as God has forgiven you in Christ.* (4: 29-32)

The season of advent is a good time to begin this discipline. In the next three weeks, try to be aware of every word you speak; every word we utter should pass through three gates, each with a gate keeper asking: *Is it true, is it necessary, and is it kind*? Our statements should meet all three criteria, not just any one of them.

None of the cases I mentioned above, the Shirley Sherrod case, or the Megan Meir case, or the death panel issue would have passed this test. None of them were true, necessary or kind.

On the other hand, there may be situations where the information is actually true, but it still won't be either necessary or even kind to share it. Let me give you a couple of examples.

The other day I found out that one of my co-workers was having an affair. It is true because he told me about it. That evening, I was having a telephone conversation with a mutual friend who is unaware of our co-worker's affair. I was tempted to tell him about it because telling others about something they don't know has certain power to it; it makes you feel important; it makes you feel that you are better than others. It has a huge ego boosting effect to it.

The information is true. But it was neither necessary nor kind to share it with my colleague.

One day, a 70 year old woman was burying her husband. After the funeral, a cousin of her husband approaches the widow and tells her that her husband had molested her when she was a child. It is a true fact, but it was absolutely unnecessary and definitely unkind to share that information with the widow after she had just buried her husband.

We might think that words don't have power. Recently I watched a *You Tube* video showing the power of words. There was a homeless man sitting on the side of the street begging for money. He had a cardboard sign that said: BLIND, PLEASE HELP. Few people tossed their coins into his bowl. Then a lady comes and turns the cardboard over, and writes another message and hoards of people began tossing money in the bowl. Instead of the words BLIND PLEASE HELP, the new words were: THIS IS A BEAUTIFUL DAY, BUT I CAN'T SEE IT.

Yes, our words matter; how we use them, matter. Christmas is the celebration of the Word made flesh. The eternal Word of God became flesh in the person of Jesus, and everything Jesus said and did, became a source of healing and salvation.
We are followers of the Word made flesh. Jesus is the eternal Word. He is not in the world physically to speak his healing, compassionate words. He wants us to do it on his

behalf.

As we wait for the birth of the Word made flesh in the next three weeks, I want you to ask one question to yourself:

When words fall out my tongue, do they become a source of healing and compassion for others or do my words create pain and suffering for others? Are my words true, necessary and kind?

Let the Word made flesh help you keep your words pure, holy and wholesome.

26. Holy Ground versus Stand Your Ground
Text: Psalms 104: 5-13

He set the earth on its foundations; it can never be moved. You covered it with the deep as with a garment; the waters stood above the mountains. But at your rebuke the waters fled, at the sound of your thunder they took to flight; they flowed over the mountains; they went down into the valleys, to the place you assigned for them. You set a boundary they cannot cross; never again will they cover the earth. He makes springs pour water into the ravines; it flows between the mountains.

They give water to all the beasts of the field; the wild donkeys quench their thirst. The birds of the air nest by the waters; they sing among the branches. He waters the mountains from his upper chambers; the earth is satisfied by the fruit of his works.

Today is *Earth Day*. The first earth day was celebrated on April 22, 1970. We have come a long way from that day with one billion people participating in *Earth Day* celebrations in 192 countries.

Usually, ministers don't preach about earth day because it is considered a "worldly" topic. A few years ago, I would not have noticed this day, or paid any attention to it, let alone preach about it. So much has changed in my spiritual life that I consider *Earth Day* as important as Christmas, Easter and other religious holy days.

It is not because I am a new age guru, or a tree hugger or an ardent environmentalist (which are usually used as pejorative terms). It is because I have reflected deeply about the unfathomable beauty, mystery and magnificence of this moving, yes, *moving* blue dot in space which holds me up as God holds me tenderly in the palm of His/ Her hand.

Today, I invite you to join me in reflecting about the earth from a spiritual point of view. I want you consider it from a divine perspective. Every Sunday, we start the service by singing, *We are Standing on Holy Ground*. We think of church as holy ground, but I want you expand your mind to include every ground as holy; the whole earth as holy because it is created by God.

Genesis 1:1 says: "In the beginning God created the heaven and the earth." That is why the Psalmist proclaims, "The earth is the Lord's and everything in it." (Ps.24.1) In Ps.102:25, the Psalmist says, "In the beginning, you laid the foundations of the earth." "Be exalted, O God above the heavens and let your glory be over all the earth. (108:5)

Thomas Aquinas who understood the deeper meaning of that psalm said: "Divine revelation comes in two volumes; Scripture and Nature." More than half of the population of this world is illiterate. They can't read or write. They will never read a bible or any another holy book, but they can look at nature and if they stop and pay attention to the earth and the universe around them, they will see God everywhere.

We usually focus our attention on the bible and look for God in the book. There is nothing wrong with it. But just for today, I like you to focus on the earth beneath you and around you to experience God.

I have lived on this earth 21,170 days and it has never failed to provide for me air, water and food, the three most basic ingredients needed for my very existence. Thank you, holy mother earth. As I walk gently on this holy ground, I join with prophet Isaiah this morning to say: "The whole earth proclaims the glory of God."

Let us take a closer look at our home planet. We usually experience it as stationary, because that is what our five senses tell us. But if we could stop for a moment and reflect, we will realize that we are moving, rather spinning, and yet staying put...that is a huge mystery worthy of adoration itself.

The earth spins around her axis at the speed of 1,000 miles an hour at the equator. It takes 24 hours to spin around once. The spinning makes our days and nights. But as we spin, we are also on another circle journey as we orbit around the sun. Traveling at the speed of 66,600 miles an hour, this second journey takes 365 days to complete. In that annual pilgrimage around the sun, we travel 595 million miles.

This moving planet is huge. But compared to the sun, earth is very tiny; the sun is 1.3 million times bigger than the earth, but compared to Antares, the 15th brightest star in the sky, which is a 1000 light years away, the sun is a pixel. **It is a mind boggling reality and miraculous magnificence combined in one unfathomable mystery that blows my mind away and fills my heart with incomparable awe.**

Back to earth; it weighs a gazillion tons, a normal calculator don't have digits for that. It is 6 plus 24 zeroes after that. The surface is 300 million square miles; there are 7.7 million species of animals living on it. We are familiar with a cat or a dog or a cow or an elephant, a donkey or a horse, but there are millions of others. There are 2700 different species of snakes. Have you ever stood in front of an aquarium and watched those beautiful fishes with different colors and textures? We might see a dozen varieties; but there are 2400 different varieties out there in the vast oceans. There are a 1000 species of birds.

And the amazing thing is that this huge earth with everything in it is not attached to anything...nothing below, nothing above, nothing in front or back, except deep dark endless space...and yet we don't fall down or spin out of control.....we don't deviate from the path...because, if we deviate from the orbit by one inch closer to the sun, we will be incinerated; one inch away from the sun, we will be frozen to death; to me that is another greatest mystery and miracle that ignites my imagination, bends my knees to the ground and opens my heart for adoration.

Just go to the beach, look at the vast ocean and endless sky and contemplate the universe and if your eyes bulge with tears, and your heart pounds with wonder and your mind feels a deep awe, you are having a spiritual experience. You are connecting with God, the creator of the universe. Such an awareness of distance, speed and order creates a sense of awe and wonder.

Astronauts who have had the privilege of seeing the earth from space were always moved by its beauty and majesty. This is what astronaut Edgar Mitchell said as he gazed down on the home planet: *On the return trip home, gazing 240,000 miles of space towards the stars and the planet from which I had come, I suddenly experienced the universe as intelligent, loving and harmonious. My view of the planet was a glimpse of **divinity.***

Perhaps what we need is a trip to outer space, to have our eyes and hearts opened to see the sacredness behind the appearances and to reawaken that inner light buried beneath our limited ways of thinking.

But, wait a minute. *We are traveling in space*; we don't have to lift our bodies from the earth to see the beauty and the splendor of God's creation; we only need to lift our minds...and open our eyes. But, that is the problem...our minds are small and our eyes are closed.

It is worthy of note that Mitchell uses the word 'divinity' not 'God'. God is a divisive term for many. Religious people fight over their definitions of God and make declarations like, "My God is bigger than your God." But, if we can speak of 'divinity' it has an all embracing quality to it. When we use 'divinity' instead of 'God' what is at work is 'spirituality' not 'religion.' And our goal should be to evolve more each day as spiritual beings not merely as religious people.

When we see the earth as a whole, from outer space, we can clearly see the connectedness and interdependence of all of us who live upon this planet. We have created imaginary boundaries, dividing ourselves into countries and states. We forget that in reality we are all living together, breathing the same air, drinking from the same water, eating food grown from the same earth.

We share everything on this planet with other people, whether we are conscious of it or not, and those people are our brothers and sisters. For example, the air that is in your lungs today was circulated yesterday through the lungs of somebody living in China. You don't have to go as far as China, but think of someone, may be a person or a group of persons you don't particularly like. You and them partake of the same air.

The air in another person's lungs is in yours a few hours later, thus establishing an invisible, but real, bond between you and that person. Celebrating earth day reminds us that we are not strangers to each other, but members of the same human family. Seeing earth as a whole brings new meaning to Christian concepts like "Communion of Saints" and "Body of Christ."

Jesus had a special appreciation for the earth. He didn't live in high rise condos or work in board rooms. He taught on the mountain top, and the seaside; he prayed in the garden, and died on a hill. He talked about the lilies of the field and the birds of the air, because Jesus knew that the earth proclaims the glory of God.

That is why this Son of God came on the earth. Jesus could have sat somewhere up in the heavens and given us his teachings, but he chose to be part of this world. That is the meaning of incarnation: God becoming flesh in the world. If God found this earth to be worthy of His attention and care and embraced it and transformed it, we too should do the same.

Don't just live on the earth as aliens and strangers, plundering and taking advantage of its resources, but be respectful and grateful for everything that the earth offers, which is our life itself. The earth can survive without us, but we cannot survive without the earth.

We came out of the earth and we will return to it. That should be a humbling thought.

So celebrating earth day is about seeing the big picture; it is about feeling the connection with the earth, with everything and everyone on it; it is about thinking about the welfare of all people beyond the boundaries our nation; it is about relinquishing narrow nationalism and embracing a wider humanity.

Earth day is about looking at all the people on this earth as members of the one body of Christ. It is about feeling the love of Jesus in our heart and walking on holy ground as opposed to holding a gun in our hand and "stand our ground." We know what that did to Trayvon Martin in Sanford, Florida.

If George Zimmerman had considered his neighborhood "holy ground," a great tragedy could have been averted. Instead, he saw the little swath of real estate he occupied, as his ground that needs to be protected by him from "others."

Earth day should remind us that there is no ground that should be barricaded and claimed exclusively as ours, because we are on the ground only for a short period of time and the earth ultimately belongs to God.

"Divine revelation comes in two volumes: Scripture and Nature." On this earth day, I encourage you to focus on the second volume! And as you leave the holy ground of this church, I pray that you consider every ground as holy and every person you meet as a manifestation of the Holy One.

27. Are You Joyful?
Text: Philipians 4:4-7

Rejoice in the Lord always. I will say it again: Rejoice! Let your gentleness be evident to all. The Lord is near. Do not be anxious about anything, but in everything, by prayer and petition, with thanksgiving, present your requests to God. And the peace of God, which transcends all understanding, will guard your hearts and your minds in Christ Jesus.

There is a movie called the *Bucket List*. In that movie, Jack Nicholson and Morgan Freeman, who are both diagnosed with cancer, are in adjacent beds in a hospital. They have six months to live, so they make a list of things they want to do before they die.

Jack is a millionaire who has a private jet. He invites Morgan to go with him and they travel to many of the historic and scenic sites of the world. The Grand Canyon, the Taj Mahal in India, and Mount Everest. They wine and dine in expensive restaurants in exotic cities. Jack even gets a tattoo.

After having done everything they wanted to do, they are on their return flight home. Jack still has to take care of some unfinished business with his daughter with whom he has not talked in years. During this flight home, Morgan is in a pensive mood and there is a powerful conversation that takes place between the two. He tells Jack, and I am paraphrasing:

You know Jack, at the end of our lives, when we stand before the judgment seat of God we will be asked just two questions. We will not be asked how much money we made, how much education we had, how many houses and cars we possessed, how many places we traveled to, or how many degrees and diplomas we accumulated. None of these things we consider important and fight hard to get, are relevant at the time of death. We will be asked just two questions, two simple questions; 1) were you a joyful person? and 2) did you bring joy to the people around you?

That is it.

Speaking of movies, I like to tell you the story of a movie critic, a very famous one. If you know the name of one movie critic in the United States, it is Roger Ebert, of Siskel and Ebert fame. These guys were famous for their *Two Thumps Up* rating of movies. Both of them worked for the *Chicago Tribune* and they had a TV show called *Siskel and Ebert*. Gene Siskel died a few years ago.

Roger was diagnosed with thyroid cancer in 2006. Instead of the traditional chemo therapy, he chose to undergo an experimental neutron radiation surgery. That surgery and two others failed, leaving Ebert without a jaw, unable to speak, eat or drink.

Since he was denied of some basic functions, he took advantage of what he still had: eyes, ears and a resilient brain and fingers to punch out brilliant prose. He published his autobiography. It is called *Life Itself*. One of the powerful themes in that book is this: *We must try to contribute joy to the world.*

He says he did not realize that early enough. He writes: "I didn't always know this and I am happy I lived long enough to find it out."
Roger Ebert is not alone in this. I think most people never

find out that they are born into this world to contribute to the joy of the world. Instead, they contribute to the pain and misery of the world. For some people, it takes a crisis, like and accident or life threatening illness, to find that out.

But why wait till the end? Why don't we start right now, today, to be an agent of joy to the world? Let us ask ourselves those two basic questions: 1) Are you a joyful person? 2) Do you bring joy to the people around you? In fact, they are not two separate questions. The second question is actually redundant. If you are a joyful person, you will inevitably bring joy to the people around you, because joy is contagious. You don't have to try hard to spread it; it will take care of itself.

So, there is only one question: Are you a joyful person? Before you answer that question, try to think of some of the joyful people you know. They live among us; you will know them when you see them. I have a lot of joyful people in my life. I will start with the first person, my wife, Judy.

She is a very positive person, always loving, caring and smiling. She has been like that for 24 years of our marriage. She has a great sense of humor too, which by the way, is one of the great ingredients of a joyful personality. If you can stop being too serious about life, and try to see the funny side of life, you will be much better off.

The other day one of the lights went out in our bathroom; Judy tried to fix it but couldn't. I went inside, pushed and pulled a few wires and voila, the light came on; I am no mechanic and I have no clue how electricity works. It was just a fluke. Incredulously, Judy asked: "*How did you do that?* And I quipped, "After all these years of marriage, don't you know that I am the light of the world?"

She came right back with a biblical response to boot: "You are also the salt in an open wound."

Last year, we were talking about old age. We both agree that if we are in a situation where there is no hope of recovering, don't prolong life with artificial means, such as tubes, bags and expensive surgeries. I told Judy that I would honor her request. And she said; "Don't put a pillow over my head or pull the plug when I get a cold; wait for a few days."

Few people speak of their spouse as a joyful person. That is why 50 percent of marriages end in divorce and in many marriages, the quality of relationship is lukewarm at best. There is a lot of acrimony and arguments in many relationships. They stay married, not because there is genuine joy, but for many other reasons.

According to a study that came out recently, divorce rate has declined in the US in the last three years, because people can't afford to divorce. They don't have the money for attorney fees and court costs; they don't have the resources to afford separate households. A not so joyful husband recently told me that he is staying with his wife for health insurance. He is covered under her policy; he does not have a job with benefits. He jokingly told me: "I am too young for Medicare and too old for women to care."

If you are married or in a relationship, you may want to ask this question to your spouse or partner: "Do I bring joy to your life?" It is a very difficult question to ask, and 99 percent of people won't dare ask it, because they don't want to hear the answer. Everybody knows the answer but nobody wants to hear it. It is a risky question to ask, but the rewards could be enormous and life changing. I encourage you to ask that question. It could improve your marriage and transform your life.

Let me tell you what it means to be a joyful person. First, I like to clarify the difference between joy and happiness. They are not the same. Happiness is usually a fleeting emotion; it is often external; it comes from possessing a lot of stuff. It comes and goes depending on the external situations. For example, I saw a bumper sticker the other day which read "I am happy today; don't ruin it." Happiness is a feeling you have when things go right or when you buy a new car. When I bought my car, I was so excited and happy for a week.

Joy is something deeper. It does not depend on outside events or circumstances. You can have a terminal illness and still be joyful. St. Teresa of Lisieux, who is called the Little Flower, fought a disease all her life. She died at the young age of 23, but was joyful. Helen Keller who was deaf and blind, was joyful. Roger Ebert, who lost his jaw, his voice, his ability to eat and drink, found out at the end, that he should make a contribution to the joy of the world.

So joy is an internal experience that has very little to do with external happenings. I like to share with you the formula for joy by explaining the three letters of the word JOY. J stands for Jesus, O stands of Others and Y stands for You.

When you have a positive relationship with Jesus, Others and Yourself, you will always have JOY.

What does positive relationship with Jesus mean? It is not

just believing that Jesus is God, and that he is your savior. All Christians basically believe that but all Christians are not joyful. If that were the case, this country should be one of the most joyful countries in the world, because we have more than 300 million Christians in this country. We may be the richest, and we may have the most powerful military in the world, but we are not the most joyful. If we are a joyful nation, we would not be engaging in wars killing innocent people. The Vietnam War killed 3.8 million Vietnamese people. According to credible estimates, the war in Iraq killed more than a 100 thousand Iraqis, not to mention the death toll on our soldiers.

So, a superficial belief in Jesus as the Lord will not bring joy to you or others. You have to get to know the real Jesus whom you meet in the pages of the gospels. The Jesus you see in the gospels is not primarily the Lord and Savior, but a real human being who went around preaching love and forgiveness and practiced them; a Jesus who embraced sinners and healed the lepers; a Jesus who was kind to everyone including his enemies; a Jesus who would dare to break the religious rules of his day by talking to the Samaritan woman and touching the leper. Knowing that Jesus, and forging a relationship with him, will bring joy to your heart and a joy and peace which neither the world can give nor take away.

The second letter of the word joy is O. You have to have a positive relationship with the people around you, starting with your immediate family, and extending that to your church, your city, your state, your country and beyond, all countries and people of the world, even the universe itself.

The other day, I heard a Tea Party member being

interviewed on TV. He said: "I care about the USA; the rest can go to hell."

That may be an extreme view, but if you have any semblance of such an attitude in the deepest recesses of your heart, you won't be joyful. It affects your primary relationship with Jesus, because in Jesus, we are all one: "There is neither Jew, nor Greek, neither male nor female, neither man nor woman; we are all one in Christ."

The third letter of the word joy is Y. You have to have a good relationship with you to be joyful. In fact, that is where it should start. Because, the commandment is, "love others as you love yourself."

Having a great relationship with you is so important. So the basic question is: "Do you like what you see in the mirror?" I am not talking about what you see with these eyes. Do you like the person you have become in terms of your relationships? Have you found your purpose in life? Is your purpose consistent with the purposes of God for you? When you wake up in the morning and put your feet on the ground, do you say: *"Good morning,* Lord", or *"Good Lord,* morning?"

Do you have a smile on your face? Okay, you may not be a morning person, and there may not be a smile on your face, but is there a smile in your soul?

Don't wait till six months before kicking the bucket to make your life meaningful. Don't let a terminal illness, as in the case of Roger Ebert, to force you to think about contributing to the joy of the world. The time is NOW.

28. Live in the Moment
Text: Matthew 6: 28-34

And why do you worry about clothes? See how the lilies of the field grow. They do not labor or spin. Yet I tell you that not even Solomon, in all his splendor, was dressed like one of these. If that is how God clothes the grass of the field, which is here today and tomorrow is thrown into the fire, will he not much more clothe you, O you of little faith? So, do not worry, saying, 'What shall we eat' or 'What shall we drink?' or 'What shall we wear?' For the pagans run after all these things, and your heavenly Father knows that you need them, But seek first his kingdom and his righteousness, and all these things will be give to you as well. Therefore do not worry about tomorrow, for tomorrow will worry about itself. Each day has enough trouble of its own.

I work as a hospice chaplain. The name of the company is VITAS hospice. *Vitas* is a Latin word which means life. Although we are in the field of death and dying, we want the world to know that ultimately, we are about life: Quality of life before death.

We go to business fairs and conventions to promote our company. Last year I was at a church fair with other vendors. We had a nice table set up with literature about *Vitas*, we had pens and mugs and tea shirts with *Vitas* written all over them. We also had a huge banner on the top that said: *Vitas Hospice.*

This nice lady walked up to my table and said: "I have a score to settle with your company." She was angry. She said that her husband was on hospice care for three months.

He is now dead and buried, but she is getting all these bills from our company and they are for thousands of dollars.

I told her that our company does not send out bills to any patient or families. If a patient is over 65 years old, Medicare covers hospice. If a patient is under 65, private insurance picks up the tab. *Vitas* does not send bills to patients or families. That is a fact, and I told her that. She got madder. She accused me of not knowing the policies and practices of my company. I was not amused; but being a professional, I did not show that. She went on and on...and finally she opened her pocket book, took out an envelope and threw it on the table: "If you don't believe me, you look at them."

I picked up the envelope, took out the bills and looked. Yes, they were medical bills. Yes, they were for thousands of dollars, yes the amount was past due....but there was a problem; a problem with just one misplaced letter of the alphabet. Those bills were from an insurance company called VISTA. *Vitas*, the hospice company; *Vista*, the insurance company; a single letter of the alphabet. Huge difference. Had she paid attention to it, a lot of headache could have been avoided that morning: the agitation, the anger, the ill feeling, the racing heart beats, the high blood pressure, and of course, the embarrassment...and the profound apology.

There is a saying that speed kills. We see it on TV on a daily basis. People going 90 miles an hour lose control of the vehicle, hit the wall or tree or a truck, and die on the spot. Life on the fast lane can drain the life out of us, emotionally, physically and spiritually.

We live in a fast paced society surrounded by microwave

ovens, ATM machines, smart phones, instant messaging, and of course, multitasking seeking instant gratification. We are so distracted and frazzled, and always in a hurry, with no time or patience to stop and smell the flowers. We become easily frustrated, and severely impatient. The lady in the *Vitas-Vista* story suffered emotional distress and embarrassment; but a distracted and hurried life can sometimes cost you financially too. Let me tell you another story.

Few months ago, I had to renew my cell phone contract and purchased a new phone. If I did not like it, I had the option to return it in 30 days, and get a new one. I wanted a fancy phone. So I contacted AT&T and they said they would send me a new phone, and I had to send the old one back within ten days in the box my new phone arrived. All that I had to do was affix the prepaid label on the box and drop it in a mail box.

The new phone arrived; I packed the other phone in the box, affixed the label and dropped it off at the UPS counter in the Office Depot in Coral Springs.

That night, I was doing my examination of conscience before going to bed, a practice I learned during my seminary days.

During this exam of conscience, I had a feeling that I was supposed to drop off the package at USPS, not at UPS. I went down and checked the paper work, and yes, it was USPS, not UPS. Just one misplaced letter, again the letter S, began to cause me anxiety and sleeplessness.

I went to bed, but I could not sleep. How foolish of me not to pay attention to the paper work. It was not just a foolish

mistake, but it was a costly mistake too.
AT&T had told me that if the old phone does not reach their warehouse in ten days, my credit card will be charged for the full price which is a whopping $299. Now, $299 is a lot of money for me. I lost more sleep that night. Carelessness can be very costly.

Next morning, as soon as Office Depot was open I went in, and rushed to the UPS counter. I thought that they would set aside the package as they cannot scan it through their system. But the package was nowhere to be found. I said to myself: "Maybe the clerk at the counter took it home because she knows it is not a UPS package; maybe the UPS driver took it home, because he cannot scan it through his system."

I was so upset as I started driving home. Suddenly, I noticed a UPS truck behind me. I thought maybe God was sending this driver behind me with my package. That would be too good to be true. I was stopped at the next traffic light and the truck pulls up next to me and I looked pleadingly at the driver. He was not looking at me. But I see this big telephone number on the side of the truck: Call 1800 PICK UPS.

Every UPS tuck has it. So, I thought I would just call them anyway. I got a nice agent on the phone. I told him my story. He said: "This happens all the time; you are not the first one doing this; our drivers are instructed to drop them off at the nearest USPS mail box."

I was so relieved; I prayed that was the fate of my packet. And I began checking the tracking number three times a day. But there was no good news because it was not tracked through the UPS system! But on the 8th day after I dropped off of the box, I got an email from ATT. The device had reached their warehouse in Texas. I was happy and relieved!

But the anxiety, self-recrimination and blaming that went on during that week was just horrible. I was not a happy person because this problem was at the back of my mind. All because of a misplaced letter *S*, all because of my carelessness and not paying attention to details and failing to live in the moment.

As an observer of life, I feel that most people are sleepwalking through life and that includes me. We don't pay attention to the details of life and savor experiences to get a full range of their impact. As hard as I try to keep awareness alive, sometimes I do things in a hurry, and make mistakes. The story I told you is one example. After that, I was very careful and began paying more attention to life. But I failed again.

I got an automated message from the library that the book I had put on hold had arrived. So I went to the Northwest Regional Library in Coral Springs. That is the library I always go to, but my book was not there! The clerk told me that it is at Northwest Library in Pompano Beach. There are three libraries in Broward County with basically the same name that unless you pay close attention to, you will make a mistake. 'Northwest' in Pompano Beach, 'North Regional' in Coconut Creek and 'Northwest Regional' in Coral Springs. When I put the hold on the book, I clicked the wrong branch because I didn't pay attention.

I did not get upset with the clerk when she told me that the book was not there. I did not blame myself for making a careless mistake. I did not get aggravated for going to the wrong branch. I took it in stride. It was a learning experience in awareness. The lesson for me is, SLOW DOWN, TAKE A DEEP BREATH, PAY ATTENTION.

Where is your mind right now? Is it here in the present, in the church? Is it in the future, with bills needing to be paid or problems that need to be solved? Or in the past, thinking about tasks that are long finished? The mind has long been regarded as a slippery beast, being compared in some yogic texts to a monkey that leaps from tree to tree, impossible to catch.

Too often, we move through our days thinking about the next thing we need to accomplish, or criticizing ourselves about something we did in the past. Far too rarely do we focus on the present, or where we are in the moment, to simply be.

Living in the moment is both simple and complex; living in the moment is about just being. Being fully present in every situation, body, mind, and soul, so that you experience everything you do, totally and absolutely.

In those moments when you engage yourself completely, nothing in the future exists--and nothing in the past is holding you back. While it might be a challenge to always be present, you can start small. As you go about your day, try to be aware of what you're doing, be it driving, reading, or even drinking water. Give your full attention to each activity.

Set aside your anxieties about next week's meeting or tomorrow's dental appointment. Listen intently to every conversation, without any expectations, without finishing anyone else's sentences, without preparing your rebuttal.

Even everyday chores warrant your full focus, whether you're writing a letter or washing dishes.

Be aware of your surroundings. Notice the color of flowers, the scent of rain, even the gum on the sidewalk. Pay attention to what is happening at every moment, and don't fight what is.

If you look at the stories in the gospels, you will find that Jesus always lived fully in the moment paying attention to the details and never in a hurry. In the story of the Samaritan woman, all that mattered was this woman at the well. Jesus did not pay attention to anyone watching him, or the disciples getting suspicious. He was with her in the moment which resulted in her conversion.

In the story of Zacheus, Jesus spotted this short man in a crowd and paid full attention to him, and his life too was changed.

When Jesus was sleeping on the boat, he was in the middle of a storm, but that did not disturb his peace because he was able to be present to the moment. When he heard the news about the death of his good friend Lazarus, what does Jesus do? He does not panic. He does not get all out of shape with emotions of worry and anxiety. The bible says, "When he heard that Lazarus was sick, he stayed where he was for two more days." Jesus is not in a hurry, not worried, not anxious, just living in the moment.

Jesus asks us to do the same in the *Sermon on the Mount*: "Do not worry about tomorrow for tomorrow will take care of itself. Each day has enough trouble of its own." Jesus is asking us to slow down and focus on each day, each moment. Be still and know that I am God.

Jesus gives the great example of the birds of the air and the lilies of the field that God takes care of so well. So there is a promise and a guarantee from God that we will be taken care of as well, if only we could just live the life that God gave us each moment and cherish it with gratitude and celebrate it with intention and attention.

29. MAGIC Formula for the New Year
Text: Matthew 5: 3-10

Blessed are the poor in spirit, for theirs s the kingdom of heaven. Blessed are those who mourn, for they will be comforted. Blessed are the meek, for they will inherit the earth. Blessed are those who hunger and thirst for righteousness, for they will be filled. Blessed are the merciful, for they will be shown mercy. Blessed are the pure in heart, for they will see God. Blessed are the peacemakers, for they will be called sons of God. Blessed are those who are persecuted because of righteousness, for theirs is the kingdom of heaven.

There is a Disney movie called *Aladdin*. What I remember distinctly about that movie is Aladdin and Princess Jasmine riding on a magic carpet, going places, singing a song of love, hope and adventure.

As we enter a new year, I asked myself if it was possible to ride the year on such a magic carpet. Is it possible to continue and sustain the happiness and joy that is wished at the beginning of the year? If we are truly disciples of Christ, there has to be a way to maintain the happiness that Jesus promised. There is a magic formula to do that, but before I explain that, let us take a moment to reflect on the year that just passed.

2009 was a bad year for a lot of people. Millions of people lost their jobs and their homes. The nation barely escaped from the brink of depression and the effects of economic collapse is still deeply felt in different parts of the country.

More than likely, it has been a year of mixed blessings for all of us. A major blessing we all share today is that we were spared of hurricanes this year. But the biggest blessing is that we are here today. Nearly 300 million people in the world, who started the New Year with us on January 1, 2009, passed away this year. I lost 134 patients on my hospice team. Bill Unch and Gail who started the year with us are not here today.

The Lord gave us a new lease on life on Friday, and the question is what are we going to do with that? How are we going to spend the next twelve months of our lives? Are we going to be happy this year, or is the happiness that is wished going to disappear in a few weeks or so, as the new year becomes an old year?

I am going to share with you a MAGIC formula to make the year happy every day of your life this year.

This is a formula that was used by men and women who really understood the meaning of life. This is a formula used by Jesus himself and is prescribed by Jesus for his followers.

The five letters of the word MAGIC stand for five words. The first is **Mindfulness.** What does it mean to be mindful or to have mindfulness? Mindfulness simply means being present to LIFE. It may sound simple, but it is very difficult to practice. Many people are not present to life. They are absent from today, because they are living in the memory of yesterday or the fantasy of tomorrow. They are frazzled, fractured and fragmented most of the time. They go through life in such a hurry that they fail to pay attention to what is right in front of them.

I take my autistic son for soccer every Saturday during the fall. Nearly a hundred disabled children are in this program. Every child has a buddy, usually a high school student who helps them play the game. It is amazing to see these children with various disabilities running and laughing and falling down trying to kick the ball. It is fascinating to watch this boy with Down Syndrome kick a ball through the goal post, assisted by his buddy, and to see his pure joy, manifested by his loud laughter and the clapping of his hands. It is a scene to behold.

But what do most parents do? They are either on their laptops, searching the web or talking on their cell phones. They are not paying attention to what is happening right in front of them. They fail to watch the beautiful drama of life unfolding before them in real time.

You can see similar scenes if you watch checkout lines in grocery stores. Most people are on their cell phones while the clerk is scanning the items. They behave as if the grocery clerk is an invisible person, a nobody. I feel like telling them to "put the phone away, return from the fantasy world you are traveling, and be present to the person in front of you."

When you are talking with someone, pay undivided attention to the person you are talking to, listen to that person fully, instead of interrupting her with your thoughts and ideas. Make the other person feel that you are fully present to her.

These are some of the ways of being mindful. When you practice mindfulness, you are fully in the present; the past and the future with its worries and anxieties just fade away.

The second letter in magic, A, is for *Acceptance.* Acceptance of life as it is, not as what you want it be. There is nothing wrong with trying hard to make life better and successful. But there are certain things you cannot change.

I have a patient on my hospice team who just celebrated her 100th birthday. About 35 people including children, grandchildren and great grandchildren gathered in a restaurant and celebrated her birthday on July 18th. The other day, I was visiting her and she was miserable and frustrated. She woke up that day, and felt confused. She did not know where she was or what day it was and she could not remember her daughter's phone number. She was very upset and began complaining: "This should not be happening to me, I don't like it, this is too hard, why is God punishing me like this?"

Another issue was that she did not want to wear diapers. "When you are 100 years old, bladder control is a problem, you better get used to it," that is what I wanted to tell her, but as a chaplain I have to be more diplomatic. This lady who is mentally alert, had no sense of acceptance of the reality of her life.

There are certain things in life that you have to accept. Aging is one of them. Death is another. Fighting against them is only going to make you unhappy and miserable. I suggest that you say the Serenity Prayer every day, in the New Year: ***God give me the serenity to accept the things I cannot change, the courage to change the things I can, and the wisdom to know the difference.***

The third letter in magic, G, stands for *Gratefulness.* Gratefulness is closely linked to acceptance. If you are an accepting person, you will be a grateful person too. They kind of go together.

Let me give you an example from my bereavement support group. This lady in my group lost her husband. They were married for 62 years. It was a happy marriage. They have 3 children, 8 grandchildren and 5 great grandchildren.

But she is devastated that her husband of 62 years passed away. He was 90 and she is 87 now. What do you expect when you become 90 years old and complete 62 years of marriage? Does *happily ever after* mean "forever young" and "forever and ever, until eternity?" What do you say to a woman who lost her husband after 10 years of marriage, or to my neighbor who lost her husband after 6 years of marriage, or to the widow of a soldier who died in Iraq, and they were married only for 8 months?

There is no guarantee as to how long we are going to live, single or married. This is where gratefulness, acceptance and mindfulness all come together. Live each day to the fullest, with mindfulness, accept what is right in front of you, and be grateful that you have it. This 87 year old lady, who is complaining about having had only 62 years of marriage, is not being grateful for what she has had.

The fourth letter in magic, I, stands for **Inclusive.** The question to ask is this: "How big is my tent? Is it a small tent that holds only a certain kind of people or is it a big tent that holds everybody? Another way of framing that question is: "Are there walls around me that I have built over the years; walls of prejudice, racism, and homophobia? Are you in favor of building a wall around the US border and possibly making it an electric fence so that we can keep the illegal immigrants out? Believe me, there are a lot of people who are in favor of such a wall, and all of them are Christians too!

I don't pretend to be an expert on immigration policy and the question is not "who do you want to keep out of the country?" But the question is, "who do you want to keep out of your heart and mind?" Do you have a heart that is deep enough to embrace and a mind that is wide enough to include everyone in your circle of concern? If the answer is yes, you are an inclusive person and that is your path to happiness in the New Year.

The most essential ingredient of inclusiveness is **compassion**. You cannot be an inclusive person without being compassionate, and that is what the last letter of the Magic, C, stands for. We know what compassion means, but let me tell you a story of true compassion. A friend of mine was coming out of Publix with a cart full of groceries. He was approached by a man who appeared to be a homeless person. He asked for a few dollars to buy breakfast at the nearby McDonalds. First, my friend said to himself:

"He must be a drug addict, if I give him money he will spend it on drugs;" but he felt bad and gave him 3 dollars. My friend got into his truck and watched the man actually going into the McDonald's. So he drove to McDonalds, saw the man standing in line for food, went up to him and gave him another 3 dollars and told him to have lunch too. Now that is a true act of compassion. That is compassion in action.

Now, we may not act out our compassion that way all the time, but we can always have a compassionate heart. When you look at the world around you, or watch news about the larger world out there, what is your predominant feeling?

Do you feel annoyed, irritated, jealous, frustrated, angry, or judgmental? It is human to feel those emotions, but do you catch yourself and say, "These feelings are unworthy of a disciple." If you can do that, you are on your way to being a compassionate person. On the other hand, if they fester in your mind and become the template of your life, you are devoid of compassion.

Jesus lived the MAGIC formula in his life. He practiced mindfulness by being totally present to the person right in front of him, be it the prostitute, the Samaritan, the leper, even the thief on the cross beside him on Calvary. For Jesus, the person in front of him was the most important person deserving his full attention and compassion. Read any story in the gospels, and you can see this MAGIC formula working in the life of Jesus.

Today, Jesus is not merely teaching us to use that formula, but EMPOWERING us to practice it. A week ago, on Christmas, we were reminded that Jesus came into the world, to EMPOWER those who accepted him. John 1: 12 says, "Anyone who accepted him, he *empowered* them become children of God."

Let the eternal Word that became flesh in Jesus on Christmas Day, *empower* us to be **Mindful**, **Accepting, Grateful, Inclusive and Compassionate.**

30. Judgment-free Zone
Text: Matthew 7: 1-5

Do not judge, or you too will be judged. For in the same way you judge others, you will be judged, and with the measure you use, it will be measured to you. Why do you look at the speck of sawdust in your brother's eye and pay no attention to the plank in your own eye? How can you say to your brother, 'Let me take the speck out of your eye,' when all the time there is a plank in your own eye? You hypocrite, first take the plank out of your own eye, and then you will see clearly to remove the speck from your brother's eye.

A drunken man who smelled like a beer sat down on a subway seat next to a priest.

The man's tie was stained, his face was smeared with red lipstick, and a half empty bottle of gin was sticking out of his torn coat pocket. He opened his newspaper and began reading. After a few minutes the man turned to the priest and asked, "Say, Father, what causes arthritis?"

The priest replies "My son, it's caused by loose living, being with cheap and wicked women, too much alcohol, contempt for your fellow man, sleeping around with prostitutes and lack of bath." The drunk muttered in response: "Well, I'll be darned," and returned to reading his newspaper.

The priest, thinking about what he had said, nudged the drunk and apologized. "I didn't mean to come on so strong; how long have you had arthritis?"

The drunk answered: *"I don't have it, Father. I was just reading here that the Pope does."*

It is a funny story, but I like to reflect on the message. In fact it has more than one message if you think about it. First, DON'T make assumptions about the people and the world around you, based on your PREJUDICES. That is exactly what this priest did. He sees this drunk sitting next to him. The priest assumes that the drunk was asking about his arthritis. His mind was not open enough to entertain any other possibility.

The priest, in his "holier than thou" attitude, really wants to teach the drunk a lesson, and that is why he tailors down the cause of arthritis to the perceived flaws of the drunken man.

Alcohol does not cause arthritis. Being with prostitutes doesn't cause arthritis. Contempt for fellow man doesn't cause it. According to American Medical Association, "determining the cause of arthritis can be difficult, because often several factors contribute to an individual developing this common problem. Some of the risk factors that can cause arthritis include genetics, age, weight, previous injury and occupational hazards."

So what the priest described as cause of arthritis has nothing to do with science. It was purely based on his prejudice.

What is prejudice? Look at the two words: *Pre* and *judge*. Judge somebody BEFORE knowing the facts. We do this all the time and often get into trouble. Let me tell you about a prejudice I had about a lady in my neighborhood.

I see her every day, sitting in the patio with a cigarette in one hand, and the cell phone in the other. She appears to be in her fifties. She is a single parent with a teenage daughter. This woman does not have a job. I have never seen her dressed up going anywhere. She has a dog, a little pooch she walks around the neighborhood.

Few months ago, she began driving around in a motorized scooter with the dog in her lap. Now I am having all these prejudicial thoughts in my mind. "She must be on welfare, milking the system. Why can't she go to work and earn a living? Why is she becoming lazier by driving around in a motorized scooter?

While I am entertaining all these prejudicial feelings towards her, I see an older man moving in with her. His huge Cadillac is parked in front. The older man is her father. Now, I am saying to myself: "The old man might be a loser too; that is why he is moving in with his daughter because he cannot afford to live on his own; or she needs his social security income to meet the mortgage and so she invited him to live with her." These are all my prejudicial thoughts, like the priest on the subway. These are assumptions based on appearance only. Because I have not talked to the lady; I don't even know her name.

Few weeks ago, I found out how wrong I was on every count. I should be convicted for first degree prejudice on all counts and sentenced to hard labor in Siberia or something.

A few weeks ago, I was coming home from work and I saw a hospice nurse coming out of this lady's house. This nurse and I work at the same hospice. I was really surprised to see her in my neighborhood. She told me that the old man who lived in the house with his daughter was on hospice care. He has lung cancer.

I saw it as an opportunity to clear some of my prejudices and so I went up and knocked on the door. Since he was a patient on our hospice, I had a good reason to visit him. I was deeply humbled by what I found out during that visit.

Yes, the old man was her father. He moved in with her not because of bad finances. In fact, he had sold his house for half a million dollars and moved in with his daughter because his wife had died a year ago. He did not want to live in an ALF although he could easily afford it. He wanted to spend the last days of his life with his daughter not only because his life was being cut short, but his daughter too had a serious diagnosis.

His daughter's name is Janice and she has multiple sclerosis. She was a high school teacher who quit working because of her MS. She had to get a motorized scooter because her legs were becoming progressively weak with MS.

At the end of the visit Janice asked me if I could be her dad's chaplain even though he was not on my hospice team. She wanted me to be the chaplain because I had been her neighbor for 15 years. I agreed and visited him a few more times before he died.

I felt like a fool when I left their house. I had judged them badly based entirely on appearances and prejudices.

Jesus says: "Do not judge." But what exactly does that mean? Jesus is not talking about the judicial system. Jesus is not talking about screening people to see if they are terrorists. Jesus is not talking about judging on *American Idol*.

What Jesus is talking about here is the kind of judging that simply condemns people. The kind of judging that wants to put people in their place. It's the judging that is critical of others and it isn't really interested in forgiving or understanding or trying to connect with the other. It's an attitude of putting people down when you think they are wrong, rather than finding ways to build them up.

The judging that Jesus is talking about here comes from the kind of person who is a fault-finder and often negative about other people who don't see things the same way they do. The kind of person who will look for questionable motives in what others do, wondering what advantage they're trying to get out of something or someone else. The kind of person who will blame other people for the stuff that's wrong in their own lives.

The judging that Jesus is talking about arrogantly assumes many things about others. And when we are convinced of our own competence, we simply judge them without intent to build any kind of relationship with or help them.

All of us need to look at that, because we have to remember that Jesus is talking to those who want to be disciples. If you want to follow Jesus, you have to look at where you are in terms of judging others. There is enough of the Pharisee in every one of us that needs us to take this seriously.

We also need to understand that when we are judgmental, we are not compassionate. We look down on people as the priest did on the subway, with a holier than thou attitude. We miss "God's heart" for people. You see, having a critical, condemning, judgmental spirit is not compatible with really knowing God in Jesus Christ. If you know God in Jesus, then you are a forgiven person. And Jesus makes it very clear that a forgiven person is a forgiving person.

Judging others is also dangerous, because the way we judge others and the measure we use is also what God will use with us. The Hindu principle of *karma* applies here—what we measure out to others will more than likely come back to embarrass us.

We may know that in theory, but just how aware are we of our attitudes, our criticism, and our judgments of others? When was the last time you took time to examine how you are doing in that department?

We say it is unfair for others to judge us because they don't know us. Do we know others enough to judge them?

That is why Jesus wants us to be very careful, whether it has to do with people's behaviors or lifestyle, weaknesses or sins or worship preferences. Be careful, says Jesus.

It is hard not to be judgmental. As humans, we are always taking the social temperature of our surroundings. We do this when we watch TV, or take a walk, drive on the road, or go to the supermarket.

Prejudicial thoughts are almost automatic. What you do with them is what counts. Do you make judgments based on them? Or do you make it a prayer for that person or persons? Catch yourself; take a deep breath; say to yourself that the person in front of you is your brother or sister. He is not a stranger. A wise man once said that "strangers are family you haven't met, yet." For a disciple of Jesus, no one is a stranger, because, all of us are members of the one body of Christ and therefore, "whatever you did to the least of my brothers, you did it to me." Remembering those words should help us refrain from judging.

Let us pray for the grace to always live in judgment-free zones.

Made in the USA
Lexington, KY
22 March 2019